"Heather Emmett is not just a clever and dedicated researcher in the somewhat esoteric field of sound design, she is also a sound designer of no mean ability in her own right. I can think of no better person to document our darker and stranger secrets. From both an academic and social history standpoint she is admirably equipped for the job."

D1613134

Rob James

Dubbing Mixer & Sound Consultant.

"We're tapping into certain issues that society is dealing with, in the same form that an individual deals with their problems in the form of dreams..."

Walter Murch

SOUNDS TO DIE FOR

Speaking the Language of Horror Film Sound

In discussion with

Walter Murch

Claude Letessier

Gary Rydstrom

Claudio Simonetti

James Bernard

Michel Chion

Antonella Fulci

AND

THE SOUND WORLD OF DARIO ARGENTO

Written by H. Emmett
Published by Flaithulach

© 2000-2012 H Emmett.
Published by Flaithulach Ltd.
Printed in England.

ISBN NO: 978-0-9563020-1-4

ACKNOWLEDGEMENTS

I would like to thank Claudio Simonetti and everyone who took part in this research especially Walter Murch, Gary Rydstrom, Michel Chion, Antonella Fulci, Claude Letessier, the Anzellotti family and all the practitioners whose work inspired my curiosity including Dario Argento, Robert Wise and Sidney Hayers.

A sincere and warm word of thanks to my parents and to the kind memory of a special friend James Bernard.

Additional thanks go to Maitland McDonagh, Ernest and Christine Moore, Jeff Moen, University of Minnesota Press, Rachel Moeller and those of you who shall remain nameless.

Goblin photos courtesy of Claudio Simonetti

Cover design & illustrations by Heather Emmett.

*"The world is scared by darkness. It is very Darwinian, in a way.
This is the story of our evolution..."*

Claude Letessier

CONTENTS

Part I

DISCUSSIONS AND INTERVIEWS

Part II

THE SOUND WORLD OF DARIO ARGENTO

INTRODUCTION

My original research, some years ago, brought the perception of Horror Film sound creation out of the realms of 'low art' and into a more serious critical arena. This original research – the first of its kind – shone light on a somewhat misunderstood art form and encouraged leading practitioners, tutors, students and viewers to focus on the more important issues of horror film sound.

This book includes a wealth of material for researchers, fans, and students alike. Much of this information has not been available before. Part One presents a section of transcribed discussions and interviews. I conducted these as part of my research over a number of years, some of which resulted from a series of 'interesting and provocative questions' about sound.[a] These transcripts serve to provide a concise but thorough and thought provoking framework of the language of Horror genre sound.

The second half of this book goes on to exemplify and explore how this simple but powerful palette of sounds and auditory devices, can be used subliminally, not just to stimulate our feelings and emotions, but also to manipulate our cognitive understanding of a given situation, action, or filmic text. I have illustrated this via a comprehensive, in-depth analysis of sound within the films of Dario Argento.

As one of the most highly regarded directors of modern horror, the films of Italian-born filmmaker Dario Argento display a significant auteur style. The use of sound in Argento's films goes beyond a simple use of sound motives, rather it has evolved into a sophisticated form of language that I will term *auditive encoding*. This can be explained as the use of auditory motives that, through the consistent use of repetition, function as signifiers that can be decoded by the viewer to reveal vital information about the filmic text. An early example of this can be seen in Fritz

Lang's *M* where the correct interpretation of an elaborate system of clues and signs leads us, eventually, to identify and capture the killer.

Whilst it is tempting to examine the use of *auditive encoding* in different genres of film, this was not my original goal. As it is part of Argento's auteur style, that he consistently used this device within his work, he presents a prime example for a case study of this technique. Whilst Argento has over a dozen films to his credit, because of the complexity with which he encodes meaning into his soundtracks, I chose to discuss just two of his works at length, although I have referenced others where I felt it important to do so. These are analysed within a framework of sound theory including Chion's construction of 'acousmatic sound', discussions with leading practitioners (including the creators of Argento's original soundtracks), references to psychological studies on classical and instrumental conditioning, archetypal dream and religious imagery, etc.

From this we shall see that, through his development of Italian *giallo* movies, Argento has developed a cognitive use of *auditive encoding* which functions to give us clues about the killer in the narrative text. This is evidenced in the way he employs a series of auditory signifiers that aid the astute viewer in revealing such information as the identity of the killer, the killer's state of mind and even the potential victims' level of immediate danger. For example, through the association he makes between the sight and sound of water and the killer, the audience comes to decode the presence of water as a signifier for danger. Furthermore, the intensity of the sound of water indicates the level of immediate danger so that the sound of running water is encoded as signifying more danger than the sound of dripping water. 'Acousmatic sound' is used by Argento as a device to delay the unveiling of the killer so that the sound of a particular *auditive* motive comes to signify the presence of a killer without him or her visually appearing onscreen. He also encodes the sound of wind to signify the killer watching potential victims. In Argento's films therefore, sound functions as an explicit form of coding. It communicates with the audience in a language of signs that afford the astute viewer an omniscient knowledge, over that possessed by the characters in the film, regarding the killer and his or her actions. It is important to note that this work is my own interpretation having analysed and researched the subject matter to a great extent and having discussed matters at length with the relevant practitioners.

"Horror films are even more extremely, primitively emotional. The feelings of fright are ancient, aren't they?"

Gary Rydstrom

PART I

DISCUSSIONS AND INTERVIEWS

Discussions with Walter Murch

Dated 2001

Heather Emmett: A while ago we discussed how it's easier to create the emotions of fear and uncertainty through the use of sound effects than it is to create the emotions of peace, joy and happiness. Can we expand a little on this with regards to the conventions of sound editing in horror and terror films? Natural elements are frequently used to represent evil and madness. In your opinion why should the sound of water and wind feature so heavily in films relating to death or vulnerability. My analysis would suggest that the Italian style uses the sound of water to represent killers and madness. In Japanese films I hear a more maternal or childhood theme for water, and yet it seems the Americans have a tendency of using water to represent vulnerability. What is your opinion on this?

Walter Murch: I'm curious. Can you give me an example of an Italian film that uses water that way?

HE: Well, we could start with Mario Bava's *Mask of Satan*, when we see the reflection of a man in a pool of water, before he is murdered. Dario Argento was influenced by Bava and I find Argento films often use water to represent the murderer, or to mark the murderer's location. More interestingly, when I dug a little deeper I found the intensity and quality of the sound varies – with for instance a killers state of mind. In your opinion, does the language of film sound differ culturally in any significant fashion, or do you feel the sound palette is more likely to be swayed by genre conventions? We could compare for instance American films such as *Seven* or *What Lies Beneath*?

WM: Right, you might also depending on how deeply you want to get into this, but you should also track down who it was that was working on those films in terms of the sound effects editors. Because they are the *orchestrators* of the sound and as much as the sounds are determined culturally by country and also by the wishes of the director, frequently the choice of sounds is left completely up to the sound editor. The director often doesn't have any idea how to use sound and so an editor for his own personal reasons *and* reasons to do with cultural contexts, will come up with an idea and for some reason it will click within a community. In Rome say, that idea will *spread* and that particular editor will use it again on some other film that he works on. So your question is an interesting one, it raises the whole issue of what cultural determination *is*. And if you break it down it is frequently simply the result of one persons decision, or the decision of a few people that then ignite and *colours in* as it were, a certain area of emotion, or a relationship between reality and the representations of reality. It then becomes a convention. You can see it happening all the time in painting. I mean how do certain forms become symbolic of certain other things? Well, it's not that a committee decides and it's not that it's so much the unconsciousness of a culture decides, those *are factors*. But frequently some person says that 'well I'm gonna have to fill in this painting, what am I going to do?' and something seems to click. The interesting thing is to see what succeeds within a particular culture and why that success happens. I know from personal experience over and over, especially in sound that there is very little direct instruction given by the director to the sound person. Most frequently, the director is acting in a reactive mode. The editor will come up with interesting stuff and the director will say I like that or I don't like that, or sometimes they are just completely neutral. So it is the director as being somebody who *chooses* sounds or has a *sound theme* – I think is one you have to be very careful with. The director frequently has very little direct input. [b]

What's interesting taking the basis of *what you are saying*, what is interesting is that there are many more *conventions* that are generally accepted for fright and horror and uncertainty or ambivalence in sound than there are for the corresponding sunnier emotions of elation, joy, satisfaction, certainty. That when a film wants to express those kinds of emotions it *rarely* uses sound...*sound effects* to achieve them and most often goes to music. Or it simply relies upon the face of the actor, or the spirit of the way the film was shot, the visuals of it, the colours and everything. I don't know what the answer is there...why the use of sound effects can be almost immediately productive of uncertainty, fear, building tension and *not* the opposite.

HE: Do you think it's because we are coded to recognise these particular sounds from elsewhere?

WM: No I don't think so. I don't know what it is but I don't think it's that, because if it's simply a question of coding, I mean the emotions of joy, happiness, satisfaction and certainty are as much part of the human experience as fright. So if it's simply a matter of coding and there was an arbitrary system – meaning somebody just decided that this means joy, sound editors over the last fifty, sixty or seventy years would have leapt at that chance. We would love to be able to express these things easily with sound effects but we can't. The palette is very limited in those areas. I'm just thinking off the top of my head now. You know certain kinds of surf sounds are used for peace and tranquility. Certain wind through trees, also used for that same thing. Birdsong is also used for tranquility tinged with happiness and joy. But those same sounds of wind and water can be used for the tranquility of death, of eternal peace, so they are ambivalent in themselves. My gut instinct is to look into the nature of dreams themselves, because films and dreams are related in a very direct way.

Statistically, certainly I know this is true in my case and I've read that it's true in studies that have been done, that the dreams that we have are from the ambivalent to the horrific. And *occasionally* we will have a dream of great peace or joy, but most often the dreams that we have are just unsettling or just curious and then obviously we have very vivid memories of having nightmares. The ambivalence of dreaming is heavily weighted toward the ambivalent, frightening end of the spectrum and only occasionally do we dream of joy, peace and tranquility. You have to ask yourself a very deep question there which is 'why is that?' Because it begins to address the function of dreams, which in a social context is to get to the function of *what is a film doing?* Because a film and in fact any kind of theatre, but film *specifically* is the way a *society* dreams. We're tapping into certain issues that society is dealing with, in the same form that an individual deals with their problems in the form of dreams, I believe. So, if that's true, if dreams generally tend to unsettle us, or even to frighten us more than they tend to make us peaceful, then that might be an indication of why there is a much greater richness in the use of sounds that also frighten and unsettle us.

HE: I suppose if we look at primitive tales and cave paintings, we do appear more in tune with our emotions of fear. Perhaps it's about perceiving a sense of danger.. if what we are saying is that we generally remember the things that frighten us the most.

WM: Well yes, that's certainly true to an extent. I'm thinking that when people wake up and you say, 'oh how was your sleep?' and you say, 'oh I had a wonderful deep dreamless sleep.' Well that's ok but why is it that they don't say 'Oh, I had the most *wonderful* dream last night'? It happens occasionally, I'm not saying it doesn't happen, but statistically much more often it's the other way around. My hunch (and this is just my opinion, I don't have anything to back it up with), is that dreams are used by us as a course correction. That when we are on course and doing what we *need* to be doing in the *deepest* sense, that our dreams are either not there at all, or they are completely neutral. But when we are *deviating* from that, when somehow we were born to be a musician and we have wound up working in a bank, there's a tension between our inner desires (some of which are hidden from us) and what we are doing with our lives. And in those circumstances the tension gets expressed in dreams of tension. It's as if the dreams are saying to us each night,'quit your job at the bank and start learning how to play a musical instrument, or if you already know how to play an instrument then start performing.' That's my gut instinct, that they become active when we are deviating from our lives path. What I mean by that is what we do in life is somehow resonating with something deep within us. And when that's not the case (and that's not the case most of the time for many of us), life is full of tension and anxiety. Because rarely is it given to us to do exactly what is deeply most rewarding to us. I don't mean what is satisfactory from a social point of view, I mean deep down.

Dreams are there to kind of nudge us back, like they are tapping us on the shoulder saying 'go over here go over there, move in this direction', if we interpret them right.

HE: You have previously mentioned 'the power of sound over something you don't see'. For me a great example of this is the original version of *The Haunting* by Robert Wise, when we are terrorised by the sound of a faceless persistent banging. Why does sound hold such power of over things we do not see?

WM: Yes. I think it's very easy in motion picture to create a dislocation between what you see and what you hear. And in this case, even if the sound is a completely neutral sound, if it is at odds with what we are looking at then there is a tension involved in that and we tend therefore to associate that sound with that tension. If I'm looking as I am right now, I'm looking at the living room of a house where I am staying and if I suddenly start to hear quite *specifically* the sound of dripping water, I won't rest easy until I know what that sound is.

Now dripping water in itself is a neutral sound, but when you put it in a context in which it doesn't match anything that we are looking at, then we are agitated and we think, if we stop to think about it we think 'that sound is making me agitated.' Well yes that's true on the one hand, but what's really making you agitated is that 'there is nothing in what I am looking at that suggests dripping water.' Therefore what is the answer to this question? 'Is my roof leaking? Am I going crazy? Is somebody playing the sound of dripping water in order to try to make me go crazy?' There are many, many answers to that question. So it's very easy because of the nature of film and sound which run on separate tracks – the image and picture are separated – it's easy to dislocate. Dislocation itself creates tension and uneasiness and that can very easily lead to fright or horror.

HE: You've got a wider range of things to play with.

WM: Yeah. There is another compensating side to that equation, if you know what I mean?

HE: Yes I do.

WM: It's easy to create a dislocation. But if I put in the sounds which are correct to the scene that I am looking at and you just think 'oh well, everything is alright' that gets a little bit back to what we've been saying about dreams. When you are doing in life what higher powers *meant* you to do with your life, those periods tend to be dreamless or the dreams are very neutral, because everything is correct. And when there is a *dislocation* between your own life, your exterior life and your inner life, then dreams tend to become agitated, ambiguous and sometimes even horrible. With the soundtrack in a film we are in exactly that same position. If I as a sound effects editor put into this scene exactly what is visually suggested by this scene, there is a kind of neutrality of 'Okay, so what? What's next?' That does not make us feel…*happy* ! Except if we have maybe suddenly taken away a dislocation. If we have arrived at a sense of everything is in its place, then we do feel a sense of relief, but only because we've *stopped* hitting ourselves on the head with a hammer!

These things themselves don't create joy, they create a sense of relief and peace only because we've stopped creating tension.

HE: Metal is also a common auditory feature in horror and terror films. Clearly war has influenced this, but does the power of metal and mechanical sounds also represent a fear of technical development? I am thinking of for instance *Tetsuo 2* from Japan and of course the *Terminator* films. Metal seems to bring some kind of apocalyptic feel. Even in context, the sound itself can make us cringe.

WM: Well I'm thinking of a scene I did many years ago in *The Godfather* when Michael (Al Pacino) is about to kill Sollozzo and McCluskey at the restaurant.

HE: I know the scene yes.

WM: So the dominant sound on the soundtrack there is the screeching metal sound of an elevator train somewhere in the neighbourhood going round a corner and getting very, very loud. And that sound comes and goes and then returns louder and goes away and then returns even louder during the course of the scene and builds up in volume until it's at the moment just before he kills the two guys. You really should see the train coming right through the restaurant it's so loud!

HE: And was it the actual screeching of the metal sound that made you choose this sound, or was it down to the environment you were in?

WM: Well now in that particular case it was decided by the environment they were in. I grew up in New York and I grew up not too far away from and elevator train track so I knew what they sounded like. And so in this particular scene Francis wanted to have this scene play without any music, because he wanted the music to come in only at the end of the scene after the murder had happened and after Michael had dropped the gun as Clemenza had told him to. There is the shooting and then there is a suspended silence where you wonder what's going to happen next and then Michael holds out the gun and lets it go and it falls onto the ground with a clatter. And that's when the music comes in. Anyway, that environment is an urban environment and when I was looking for a sound that would presumably come from outside *wellll* maybe I could have had police sirens or maybe I could have used the sound of a large truck going by, but somehow they had other associations. Whereas the elevator train is something that has a very long arc to it. It approaches from far away and it gets closer and closer and then it disappears off into the distance and as it does (now this is the very interesting thing about metal sounds), is that the dynamics within the sounds shift very dramatically during their approach, at the point they are nearest to the microphone and when they go away. All you have to do is think what a train sounds like from very far away, up-close and then in the distance. You *hear* all kinds of different things at each stage, so there is a wonderful sense of *development* in the sound.

HE: And is this the same in terms of mechanical sounds?

WM: This is also true in my experience (in the helicopters in *Apocalypse Now*) that the *spectrum* of sounds that stretch over the course of the helicopters approach and pass-by and then receding into the distance. There is a great amount of colour in that and the colour shifts. That is something that's wonderful to work with. Whereas a sound that really doesn't change its nature as it gets closer, it just gets louder and louder and then goes away, it diminishes in sound – is a less interesting sound. It isn't (if you want) a *musical* sound because there isn't this articulation of its inward parts. And in general, sounds of nature tend to be sounds of one place. Nature doesn't move around a lot. I'm trying to think now...volcanoes erupt and the lava goes down the mountain. Animals make sounds and maybe if a lion was running at us and then in the distance. But it's not as dramatic as these *human* made *metallic* objects. First of all they are very loud. Second if all their volume is sustained over a long period of time you can hear all the different colours in them. So it's mostly that we as sound effects editors are looking for *instruments* in our orchestra and *metallic* instruments are very good. They work well because of all this great shift in tonality. So in terms of the sound itself, it's unsettling for two reasons. It's unsettling because it's so loud..and you kind of know where the source of it is. So we're in the Bronx, New York. It's 1948 and if you know anything at all about that *world* you know that there were these train *sounds* around. Now a lot of people looking at film have no idea of those things so I don't know what it *sounds* like to them. But there is a dislocation simply in terms of its loudness. 'Why is that so loud?' Well, what happens is that you take that sound (and a lot of people don't even hear that sound at all, they just accept it as being part of the environment – the given environment) and the emotions that it's churning up are given to the main actor Al Pacino and we understand in quotes, we understand this as being the sound that Michael's – the kind of sound of his brain as he's about to commit his first murder. So, the *inner* tension in Michael is expressed outwardly as the tension of this sound, that on the face of it doesn't belong in this room at that loud level. Then the other aspect of it (that just naturally tends to tension) is this low rumbling quality. There is also this high screechy sound of the wheels, the brakes of the train and those frequencies themselves do tend to set people's teeth on edge or make them feel kind of funny in their stomach.

HE: Like a musical device with low strings and high registers.

WM: Right.

HE: So by using the environment you were are able to pull out certain frequencies that put people on edge. In musical terms, we would perhaps turn to semitones and extreme instrumental registers, but are there any particular relationships between frequencies in sound that you consider particularly emotional...that you would specifically turn to, to create fear and tension?

WM: Well in the case of that, the metal screeching...it's a lot of very prominent, *dissonant* high frequency sounds. If brakes made a pure sound (WM sings a perfect F), if there was not this *distortion* in the *harmonics* of the sound, I don't think it would produce quite the tension that it does. But by nature I think of the way our brains are constructed, we are *disturbed* by these frequencies that should be closer than they are, but aren't. So if you play semitones very quickly at a high register like Bernard Herrmann used in the murder scene in *Psycho* and well yes in a sense I was doing sort of the same thing with the sound of the train in the *Godfather*. We could cite many more examples of this, it's an open question in music, why certain sounds should be pleasing to us and other sounds displeasing to us. It's an open question, nobody really knows, there are theories about it but it's a question in music theory and it's even *more* of a question in the use of sound.

HE: Although we may perceive sounds (signifiers) subliminally, I think we are conditioned to respond in a particular way to a given sound. This being the case is it possible to read a filmic text by means of the conventions used within the soundtrack?

WM: Well, when we are in the womb we live in a very rich, sonic environment. That the ear is connected to the brain somewhere around four and a half months of conception. So halfway through our life in the womb we begin to hear, and it happens that the environment we are in is a very rich, sonic environment. We hear our mother's heartbeat, we hear her breathing, we hear her voice, we hear the gurgling of her intestines. We hear that heartbeat, the gurgling twenty-four hours a day! That is there all the time and in addition we hear her voice when she is awake and we hear the voices of other people and the sounds, music, other things that are coming from the exterior environment. But we have no other senses active at that time to relate these sounds to. We're blind, we cant really feel anything tactiley, everything is very slippery. It's certainly nothing like the world would be outside where things are rough and where things can prick you. All of these textures don't exist in the womb. Taste also is not present. Smell certainly is not present, so hearing is fully active and has no competition in the womb.

HE: And these particular sounds from the womb, which we heard twenty-four hours a day, these are sounds that feature heavily in horror film soundtracks. Water, breathing, voices we cannot see...I'll keep digging.

23

WM: Yeah, yeah. No I think there is something to be said about that. Yes, keep digging! I mean they are *essential* sounds. They are essential elements of our psychic life. They were present at the very start of our consciousness, before we even knew what *we were* these sounds existed. The heartbeat, the breathing, the gurgling, the *water* sounds…and by gurgling intestines we *understand water.* So yes, *exactly* what you are talking about!

Yes, then when we come to consciousness and there is no doubt that the child in the womb is a conscious being. We used to think that these children lived in a kind of coma but in fact their brains are very active. They've done EEG studies of the child's brain in the womb and it's very clear from sonogram studies and MRI studies that when you play certain sounds, the child reacts to those sounds in a conscious way. So the child is actively *processing* sound and like any consciousness, I am assuming trying to make sense of the world out of the only elements that are being presented to the child, which is our sonic elements. Then of course this huge shift at birth you are plunged into. Your eyes open up and you are suddenly exposed to the world of great variation and texture, touch, smooth, soft, rough, sharp, dull…pressure. All of this begins to have a great deal of meaning to the child. Smell kicks in and you can hear more distinctly. Sounds have a greater distinctness when they are carried through air than when they are carried through water. But I think (and this is my own private theory) that if in the womb, those three sounds – the *cessation* of those three sounds; the hearbeat, the breathing and gurgling, their cessation can only mean one thing, which is the death of the mother. If the heartbeat stops or if the breathing stops, or if the gurgling stops, this means…'mom is dead'.

I mean when you are in the womb you don't even know there is a mother yet. So it's hard to talk in direct terms because we cant ask the child what did you feel when your mother died and these sounds stopped, because likely as not the child is going to die as well in that case. Although there are some exceptions about children who have been given birth from a mother who has died, that does happen. I know that we have spent as mammals and as primates, billions of years directly connected to our mother, even after we are born. And so these sounds of the heartbeat and of breathing and of gurgling, continue after we are born and this is a sign that there's a source of some reassurance, because we can relate our past experience to our present experience. What has really only happened within the last 150-200 years though is this practice of taking the newly born child and putting it in a separate room in the dark away from the mother. Up to two hundred years ago this was generally not the case. The newly born child slept with the mother and father in the bed. They didn't separate the child until many, many years later. So the child's experience of the world in a way was not very much different after birth than before birth. Well certainly in the twentieth century and in the nineteenth century…this idea of 'now the child is born it will have its own room and sleep in the dark.' Imagine how that *feels* to a child! A child maybe asleep lets say, but what happens if it wakes up in the night in a dark room? It opens its eyes, it doesn't know that it has opened its eyes but experiences darkness and let's say the child has an internal dialogue and the child says,"Oh! It's dark! That means I am back there again, I'm back in the womb where things were dark." But then suddenly it's a very unsettling thing because, "if it's dark and I'm back there, I should hear the breathing, the heartbeat and the gurgling..and listen! I don't hear any of that and I just hear horrible silence….WAAAAAAAAAAA!" Right? And what happens is the mother or father comes into the room, picks you up and suddenly there is the breathing, voices, gurgling, heartbeats. Everything comes back again and you gradually go off to sleep."Okay, thank God, it's back." And then you are asleep and your parents put you back and try to creep out of the room, but then there's a little noise that wakes up the child the child looks up and "Oh no! It's quiet again!" So they scream.

HE: Do you think this is along the lines of what we discussed previously? That we're afraid of things we cannot see?

WM: Yes. In a way it's the same equation but turned on its head. When we are in the womb the things that have been present from even before we were conscious are the sounds of breathing, heartbeat, running water, gurgling, sounds. They are there all the time and yet we don't know what causes them.° We have no idea, they are just part of the universe. It's only when we are born that we gradually begin to relate sight to certain types of sounds – that we *gradually* come to understand that these sounds were produced by our mother. Her voice…certainly very soon after birth, the child will respond to the sound of the mother's voice and that's because it heard her all the time when it was in the womb."Oh, there's that sound again." And the child looks and sees the face of the mother and comes to understand that this voice is coming from *her*.

This almost profound realisation about self and the world, begins at that point, which is that *that* sound, which I thought was part of the universe... is actually coming from a separate entity from me. And you understand this more and more as the months go by after birth. That your mother is somebody who *can come and go* and the voice comes and goes with her and she is *separate* from you. But you didn't begin that way. You began when you became conscious in the womb. This voice was just a part of *you*, it was part of the *universe*. And so this idea of *separation*, that this voice is something that's *not* part of you and it can *go away* and it can come back along with the heartbeat and the breathing and the gurgling-there's a very rich vein to be explored there I think.

HE: So to follow your train of thought, Carl Jung? Dream and maternal instincts? Do you follow that train of thought when you are working?

WM: I mean I remember Jung talks about dreams in some of the same ways that I've been talking about them. I think I probably got that from reading Jung – this idea of dreams and tension. I think in his autobiography he talks about that. The relative paucity of dreams of great joy and happiness compared to the dreams of tension. It was his view I think that dreams are there as a corrective measure. That when you don't need to be corrected dreams tend to either fade away or not be memorable, or to be (if they are memorable) to be simply neutral. So I mean I *use* that in a general vein when I am thinking of a sound, of *ideas* of sounds for a film.

At least, as it's experienced from inside, from the *making* of the film, the role (in general) the role of the director is not a big force in the *thinking* up of the sounds. In general directors don't have a vivid idea of the sounds of the film in advance and so in general the work is left up to the people who are *creating* the soundtrack.[d] The director can say 'I want tension here' – you think up how to do it! So that the general instructions from *where* to do things are perhaps adjusted by the director, but then the actual *implementation* of *what to do* is more often than not left up to the people who are doing the sounds. And they will sometimes forge new territory, but other times they will simply do what's worked in the past and try to reinvent it in a slightly different way. I know I've been guilty of that myself. So people – their habits and patterns tend to form as a result of this. But there is certainly not, at least not on the *surface*, nobody says in any conscious way say for instance 'Oh we're Italians we have to have water when we're seeing the murder'. This is certainly determined by *somebody* but it's not, I don't think it's determined in a *conscious* way by the society.

HE: So do you think it's more of a genre question than a cultural one?

WM: Not only *genre* but who worked on that film. Who were the sound editors on that film? Try to trace their work over the years.

HE: What's interesting to me is that people are using the same devices but aren't really aware of it...'It just worked'.

WM: Yes, yeah that's the question, when they say 'I don't know what I was doing but it worked' – then you *do* get into the realm of what is *culturally* determined because what works for one society may not work for another and that is interesting. But then there are obvious things such as what we have been discussing, which are common to all humanity. That we *all* are born and we *all* experience the mother's heartbeat and the breathing and the gurgling. Every single person on earth alive today has experienced this, so there are things that are *culturally* emphasised in each culture.

Interview with Antonella Fulci

Dated 2001

Heather Emmett: I am presently following up some ideas and comparing the sound palette used by practitioners in horror films and researching how this might have developed or been influenced by cultural or personal beliefs etc. There is some information about your father's work [Lucio Fulci] on the internet but nothing that gives me the insight I am looking for. I hope you will be able to help me build a better picture. I am interested in any spiritual or religious beliefs your father had and how this might have been relevant to his work. Was he by any chance heavily influenced by dreams, or dream theories?

Antonella Fulci: For him dreams and reality were the same. Once he lost his driver's license (I was about twelve, so it was 1972-73) and the next day he told me that Grandma Lucia came in dreams and told him where to find it. We went there and it was true. It was close to the sidewalk not far from where we lived. As a kid, this thing impressed me a lot. He was very unconventional as a person and hated conventions.You can see in his films that usually the conventional people and the bigot people are characters that he doesn't really like. He was really scared of occultism and stuff like that and very superstitious. This may seem strange but he never read a book about those things because he thought it brought bad luck.

HE: Eyes are a big feature in Italian Horror. Could you share your father's views on this? *The Beyond* is a striking example. Why on this occasion did he focus on blindness?

AF: He thought that when ones dead and on the other side, eyes become useless because you acquire an inner view. Once he answered a question about the blind girl of *The Beyond* saying she was like Virgilio in Dante's *Divine Comedy*, but I'm sure he was joking. He was terrorized by blindness himself and as a diabetic he knew that he could have later complications with his sight. Maybe even this had a role. Instead, concerning the split of the eye of *Zombie*, I always thought that it was a heartfelt and ironic tribute to his beloved Luis Bunuel and his *Chien Andalou*.

HE: What and who were your father's main influences (directors, musicians, artists etc)? And in your opinion, which filmmakers have been most influenced by Fulci's films.

AF: Luis Bunuel, Edgar G.Ulmer and Hitchcock of course...but most of all Steno (Stefano Vanzina), a maestro of Italian comedy who taught my father how to make movies. From time to time I hear that a director declares he's been influenced by Fulci – it seems a very hip thing to say. On the gore front, recently Matthew Kassovitz said he's been inspired by Fulci's atmospheres in his *Purple Rivers*. I heard many people say that *The Hidden Truths* is nothing else than a copycat of *The Psychic*. Obviously another one is Quentin Tarantino, and almost all the directors of the underground scene. After all, what gore is better than Fulci's gore!

About music, he was a jazz fanatic, jazz in all its expressions influenced him a lot.

Interview with Michel Chion

Dated 2000

Heather Emmett: Could we call the human sounds we repeatedly hear in *Suspiria* the 'maternal voice' although they do not speak words?

Michel Chion: That is a good question – some of the sounds made by the human body are gendered and personalised, for example, 'er...erm' whereas the breath on the other hand isn't. And what do we call the voice? Some sounds are almost anonymous, neither gender specific nor personalised, so we can't say who it is or whether it is a woman or a man.

HE: Even though the voices represent 'Mother Suspiriorum' and her coven of witches?

MC: One must be attentive to how a voice sounds. How does the voice sound to someone who doesn't know it is the mother? What does one actually hear?

When one watches a film one must forget what one knows and ask, 'what can I hear?'- because hearing is not rational. In my presentation on *2001*, I said that rationally the breathing is Dave's, but acoustically we don't know.

HE: In Argento's films he uses sound to signify the presence of a killer, or to tell us a murder is about to happen. I have called this device 'auditive encoding' as I have been unable to find a theoretical description of it. Would you agree these repetitive sounds are functioning as codes and clues?

MC: Yes. Everything can be coded like Pavlov; an association between two different things, if repeated, becomes a code. Films are able to create associations as in life, so when one element is repeated the other is expected. If it is just sound the question is what is it associated with?

HE: In your opinion, why are the sounds of nature used to represent killers?

MC: Nature sounds can suggest something archaic, inhuman.

HE: And water?

MC: In some cases water can suggest purity, childhood – it all depends on the context. Water is often associated to something maternal; it is life and death at the same time. Keep in mind the ambivalence of the sound of water; it is at the same time life and death.

HE: In your opinion, why is the use of repetition such a feature in the horror film?

MC: The repetition of something in cinema is often related to death – often the repetition of a sound. So, for example, in Brian De-Palma's *Blow Out*, you hear a sound like that of an insect, once again, then again ten minutes later. It is repetitive, something mechanical. The fourth time, at the end of the movie, you see a man, a killer, winding a piece of steel wire.

The suggestion of death was created by the repetition, because the sound is repetitive itself, and each time a murder is committed we hear this sound repeated, an exact repetition. It is frightening because of the repetition. Water can be heard in many forms – dripping, for example, but the way it is repeated is important, not only the symbolism of water.

HE: Because horror is less concerned with realism, sound is often dealt with perhaps more imaginatively.

MC: Yes, sure.

HE: There is more freedom to create and experiment with sound.

MC: Yes, exactly.

HE: Do you think because of this lack of *need* for realism that the horror sound track has become influential in other areas of film and media? Particularly in animation and games where there is often a very strong 'rendered' acoustic style?

MC: The sound in so-called horror film has changed a lot. If someone talks about a horror sound, or a western sound, or a cop movie sound or a sci-fi sound, that in my opinion is a historical error. A film can seem like a horror film, because it is classified in that way, because there are two or three scenes of horror. But the sound can be treated in a different way. Certain Bergman films, for example, *Hour of the Wolf* is like a horror film. He is not considered a maker of horror films but he uses the same effects. The horror film is a very rich field.

HE: Sound and music frequently cross the line. In Argento's films the composers provide much of the sound motives. Some sound designers create musical 'scores'. Should we still distinguish between sound and music, and if so how?

MC: The musical use of sound is an ambiguous idea...What does that mean? No-one really knows what it means. Anyone can say 'PSSSSCHHHT' that's music. I make *musique concrete*, I say it's music, no-one can disagree with me, but someone can say 'I don't hear it as music'. In certain films, if we hear sound with regular rhythms, we think 'Oh it's like music'. What makes us perceive a sound as like music is two things...rhythmic organisation...so we can say, 'JJJJJJ', cars passing 'JJJJJJJ JJJJJJJ' becomes music. In certain places there is a repetition and sometimes it is as if a melody draws itself for the ear. Cinema is cinema that's just the beginning, why does a sound need to be music? It's the sound of the film, that's all, why do we need to compare the sound of the film to music as if to ennoble it?

A war movie can be compared to music, not just because of the sound, but the rhythm of the performers, the editing, is like music or dance. What is more important in a film is the organisation of the rhythm, not just the sounds but in the images too. You must be sensitive to the whole organisation of the movements in the image and sound – it is like music or it is like dance – that's a good comparison. In my opinion, as I have written many books, sound cannot be separated from the images by an abstract decision because when you have rhythm in the image and rhythm in the sounds they are combined like in music. In Tarkovsky's films you often have at the beginning a very long tracking shot. In *Stalker,* very quiet and long tracking and the sound of a train passing – the whole is music, why? – because the long slow tracking shot is the perfect equivalent of a drone, a sustained bass note.

The comparison of cinema with music, with sound is good, but you must not separate the image from sound. It's the whole. When you are studying a movie you are not studying how it was made, you are studying the whole. The question of who made the sounds, who made the image, has no moral importance in my opinion. The film is the film. It doesn't matter who did what. A work is a work. The musical use of sound doesn't interest me. It's like comparing the images in a film to painting. What is important is the cinematic use of sound. A film is a whole.

Music in film is not to be considered as music but as sound. When you have music in a film it is not music in itself, you have the sound of the instruments recorded. For example in *North By Northwest* by Hitchcock the music moves us very much, not just because Bernard Herrmann was a great composer, in my opinion, but also because the recording of the sound of the orchestra is beautiful. It is beautifully played and recorded. It's like a picture; you don't have the music, you have the recording of the music by Bernard Herrmann, played by good 'cellists and beautifully recorded and mixed. And I was wondering, why am I so touched by a very simple chord in this film? The sound is moving because it is interpretation mixed and recorded. I would suggest that in talking pictures we have to consider music as recorded sound, as played, performed sound. That is also important. Something concrete, the sound of a voice, drops of water, of Herrmann's music is also a sound.

HE: I was interested to hear you speak about the use of sound in *Scream*. Do you think critics and theorists generally look down on horror genre films and indeed the use of sound in the horror film?

MC: In France I know Argento is well respected by film students. Yet in France comedy (as a genre) is not really respected. I think it could be a cultural thing. I do not know of any books that deal with sound in the horror film, or that discuss the use of sound in Argento's films, although as I say in places, *as a director*, he is very well respected. You should write the book and be the first. It is yours!

"I actually prefer not to do any music under dialogue, but sometimes you have to do things against your will...If a dialogue scene is well acted, which in those cases I think they were I must say, well then I tend to think, why do we need music?"

James Bernard

Interview with Claudio Simonetti

Dated 2000

Heather Emmett: The witch theme in *Suspiria* originally occurs with the appearance of the first victim in the woods and recurs to signify other murders in the film. How did you create this unusual drum sound?

Claudio Simonetti: The drum sound was played by an Indian tabla with a Minimoog bass sound together.

Goblin 1977

HE: The victim's eventual death is by hanging. Is it possible that this sound (like that of ropes under tension) influenced Argento's decision about the murder weapon? I read that you created the music before he filmed *Suspiria*?

CS: No, all the music we wrote was made especially for every scene of the film, and we always wrote the music when the film was shot, so the weapon was chosen by Dario *before* our music. We changed some things during the final editing of the music but more or less all the music was written and used for its scene.

HE: Often your music is so closely related to 'sound design' that we are unable to define between the two. *Suspiria* is a clear example of this. What kind of devices did you use to achieve the effects in *Suspiria*?

CS: We did the effects blended with the music. It's a part of the music, for example with the wind. The wind you hear in *Suspiria* was made by a Minimoog. Sometimes we mixed it with strange noises, for example, the crushing of a plastic cup in front of the microphone, and sometimes we blended this with the whispers. And so the noise became part of a music, the music part of a sound!

HE: Does the breathing and sighing throughout much of *Suspiria* represent the witches' all seeing and all knowing presence?

CS: Yes. That was a Dario request. He said the audience always had to feel the witches' presence during the movie.

HE: What was the instrumentation in *Suspiria*?

CS: We used instruments like Celesta, Acoustic guitar, Drums, Indian Tabla, Bass guitar, Minimoog, Moog System 100 (the big one, the one Keith Emerson used), Mellotron, Hammond organ, Clavinet and special 'hand made' effects like those used to create the human whispers and witches' sighs.

I think that the *Suspiria* soundtrack is the best work we ever made for film. The best Goblin sound to me!

Claudio Simonetti & Goblin on video in Simonetti's studio, Rome.

Interview with Claude Letessier

Dated 2010

Heather Emmett: What drew you to study psychoacoustics before going into sound design and how has that influenced you as a film sound practitioner?

Claude Letessier: I have always been curious about the genetic aspect of our understanding of our aural environment and it definitely helped me to understand the subtleties of tones/ sounds/ perception and work around those areas.

HE: Can you expand on what you mean by the 'genetic aspect of our understanding'?

CL: Prey we were. We needed to carefully understand our sound environment to hunt and survive. Ears are 360. Depending on the strength of the wind and its direction you could hear a herd approach from miles, leading to hope or fear, depending on where in the food chain you would place yourself. Beyond that simplistic explanation, ears would also help our inner sense of orientation. Please review: *Nietzsche/music: art de la penombre et des tenebres.*

HE: Who (or what) influenced you the most as a sound designer?

CL: Jerome Bosch, Pierre Henry, Xenakis, Luigi Nono, Pierre Schaeffer...

HE: What devices/sounds do you find the most productive for creating an atmosphere of fear and tension and what sound effects would you choose to release that fear?

CL: I have no idea. It is linked to the picture, the story, the drama, the text, the subtext, the music, what comes before the scene and what follows the scene. Cheesy editorial tricks always work but they are generally pretty gross..bringing all the sounds down...creating a bit of silence...and then WHOOOMPH! Big sound...pffff...shoot me, please!

I have no pre-made tricks. I really follow the arch of the movie and the elements discussed previously, for instance silence can be an option but it doesn't always work, Germans hate silence in the M&E! This means you always have to come up with some sort of artifact. Again, this is linked to the 'dramaturgie'. Does Hannecke need sound design in the *White Ribbon*? He doesn't even have score, so it is really a matter of context/ director/ style and intelligence.

HE: Silence is important in the Horror Film.

CL: Because it throws you back at a period of your life when you were in your crib, scared to death by all these shadows on the ceilings and walls and your trying to call for help but no sounds are coming out from your mouth. Remember those days?

HE: Why do Germans hate silence in the M&E?

CL: When it comes to 'normal' movies, silence, I mean dead silence, is a sign of a technical problem and they reject the M&Es. I am sure you ran into that problem before?

HE: You have worked in many countries with many 'cultures', what other cultural differences have you come across in your sound work?

CL: Well about *German* movies, or at least one German film-maker, to me it is about the "filmmaker" himself!

We are universally making big mistakes. Usually Foley is way too loud, where in the world do you hear those footsteps from across the street in a busy city?

Really, sounds follow what you see. The difference might happen in what I call the *interscore*, the tonal layer that lives between the 'real' sounds, the dialog and the score – the one that has more of the 'subliminal' approach, the more emotionally 'manipulative', the one that is there but that one should not *hear*, and usually the one that conflicts with the music, tonally and rhythmically.

I must say that there is a strong interaction with the art of mixing! A bad mix with a bunch of cool sound ideas kills the sound ideas. Making the right mix choices can bring a couple of lame sounds to a great level.

HE: In your opinion why do the sounds of natural elements feature heavily in horror film soundtracks?

CL: Because we are all afraid of being lost at night in the forest. Those "big bad wolf" stories, trauma. Our fear of darkness; it's genetic! It's the time when predators come out to catch you!

HE: Do you find this is the same universally? I mean that the same sounds scare us the world over...The same sounds calm the storm etc.?

CL: In a world of moviegoers, I would say yes, regardless of where they are coming from. The world is scared by darkness. It is very Darwinian, in a way. This is the story of our evolution. Now some of us can be more or less comfortable with darkness, but still, it goes back to us being "prey".

HE: People can be scared of what they hear but don't see. Do you have any thoughts on this?

CL: Again it goes back to connecting with our inner fears. Losing your mum and dad, not knowing where you are, fear of dying, all of these things have their aural representation attached to them.

HE: Have you been allowed a great amount of creative freedom when creating soundtracks or do you feel that directors and producers often stifle creative sound?

CL: Yes.The problem often comes from the fact that there can only be ONE 'creator' on the project and that is not...you! It is the director. So when there is dialog, there is hope but when the director has strong ideas, well you are in hell because you are becoming a 'vendor', or at least a person who executes someone else's vision, which for me is extremely frustrating. That is the nature of our job, I guess.

HE: When you worked on the *Mothman Prophecies*, who chose the sound palette and how much was decided by the director? What influenced those sounds?

CL: That was a perfect example of GREAT dialog with a crazy, cool, creative director! I never had so much fun working with a director and he kept pushing me more and more. I would come up with a palette of tones, textures and sounds and he would give a name to each of them so we could remember them later. That would allow him to, two months later, ask for the *green* sound.

HE: Were they random names?

CL: Yes, they were random names, just easy to remember, we gave fun names to those sounds. I created an aural alphabet and together we created words and sentence: fascinating. Nothing really influenced those sounds; I just let my intuition and inspiration follow the flow of the story, the cut, the FX, the narrative structure and the director's reaction to some tonal combination. It was the biggest sound playground I have ever been in.

HE: Did you work alongside the music score or was it left until the mix?

CL: Well, I came on board very early in that project and created most of its tonal web before the composers started to work, which irked them because I came up with so much tonal shit. I know it didn't make their work easy, but in the end, they had to blend and work around my sound, because it was already in place and worked pretty well against the pictures…and made the director happy!

HE: Why is it that metallic sounds work so well in horror films?

CL: Knife. Metal is blade. Knife…death.

Interview with Gary Rydstrom

Dated 2001

Heather Emmett: I would think your approach to sound is pretty much instinct driven, but there must be times where the genre of a film will stipulate certain conventions (for want of a better term), or perhaps precise expectations that you must adhere to? For example, the sound of wind often appears to indicate the presence of someone or *some thing*, or to create the impression that somebody is being watched. One example of you doing this can be found in the remake of *The Haunting*. You gave the wind a very human quality – an indication of the hidden life within the house? Again we encounter the sound of wind when there is a presence of someone being watched. In your opinion why should the sound of wind be such a common metaphor for such purposes? In the case of *The Haunting* we hear the sound of wind indoors – misplaced, but this is not always the case. I've noticed that water is a common theme for death, or it's used to identify a killer (this is most apparent in Italian Horror films) – at the moment I am pursuing the thought purity and nature turned against us. What are your own thoughts on this?

Gary Rydstrom: You're right, first of all, that I am instinct-driven. As much as I am given to analyse sound, the basic tool we all have when we do this work is our own gut reactions to sound and to the movie. I think of film as primarily an emotional medium, and I find myself always gauging my own emotional responses to sounds when making them or choosing them. Horror films are even more extremely, primitively emotional. The feelings of fright are ancient, aren't they?

What scares us are sounds we can hear but not see, or not identify and sounds that seem to be *alive*, or sounds that make us feel helpless.

There are plenty of winds in *The Haunting*, particularly in cracks through doors and windows (an unsafe feeling), but most of what sounds like wind was an attempt to make the house *breath*. We used slowed down bellows, slow human breaths through tubes, and airy blows over water bottles to make this deep, deliberate *breathing* presence for the house, giving a sense that we are being watched. But it was important to have sounds that were unclear, that could be wind, or breathing.

The unknown itself is unsettling. There were winds for the ghost children coming into the bedroom that were meant to sound alternately like wind, drapes blowing and children's whispers. That film was full of these fun possibilities for sounds that could be different things. 'Was it a pipe groan or a man, wood creaking or an animal?'

Your thoughts about natural sounds misplaced fits this idea of sounds that could be different things. As for water I can only speculate that since water is not our natural surrounding-hard to breath in and all-that it is threatening. Then, of course you have the long history of scary shower and bath tub scenes in movies such as *Psycho* and *What Lies Beneath*, which is more about our vulnerability.

HE: Another feature of your sound design is this strong focus on rhythm. What other devices do you tend to use to create tension and fear?

GR: Rhythm is important. When the T1000 is coming for us, he doesn't break stride, he is on a single track with a singular goal, so something as simple as the pace and sound of the footsteps help.[e] The T1000 music signature does the same thing.

The T Rex approaching in *Jurassic Park* also uses this methodical, inevitable pace when his boomy footsteps can be heard coming toward us. Of course, then there is the frightening pause between the last footstep we hear (he is very close), and his big appearance. Horror, like comedy, plays with our expectations with its use of rhythm, to create movement and surprise. A nice tense scene in *Terminator 2* is Sarah's escape from the mental institution: the T1000 methodically searches her out, while she struggles with a paper clip in the door lock. The sound is full of quiet tension and shocking releases. Quiet, in general, adds to tension, and makes those explosive moments of big sounds all the more shocking. Both *T2* and *The Haunting* build to chase scenes, which to me aren't tense anymore, just energetic or thrilling.

My favourite scary moments are those quiet moments before the storm, in the *Jurassic* movies as well. We are most scared when we don't know what's coming next. The scene in *The Haunting* when the two women hear strange noises moving through the walls and out into the hallway is great. The original movie by Robert Wise made much more use of these moments – the 'what the hell is behind the door' moments. To my mind, when we show more visually – which we do these days – the tension is lost. Nothing against visual effects, but to me all these movies work best when we don't see the threats. Think of the raptors attack in the long grass in *Lost World*. That's my cup of tea.

HE: Are there any particular frequencies of sound that you consider build tension, emotion?

GR: Well, it probably doesn't relate one to one between frequencies and emotions, though I certainly made use of low frequencies in *The Haunting* to make it ominous, threatening, big. I think our emotional responses to sound come from cultural contexts; why is a door creak scary? Why can crickets be soothing? A storm wind through leaves warming? The next step is to think about the relationships between frequencies.

Just as in music, the interrelationships of tones make us all respond differently. Frequencies can be dissonant, or harmonic. When trying to figure out the dinosaur voices for *Jurassic Park*, I read about animal communication, and a lot of meaning can be conveyed by whether a voice is tonally pure, or complex, in musical steps, or atonal, whether it sweeps up, or down etc. Animal communication is an interesting place to go to research why different types of sound mean certain things. Our primitive brains do a lot of our listening, I think.

In another e-mail you mentioned looking into differences of approach in different countries. I once heard that *Terminator 2* was being used in a class in Europe (don't remember where) as an example of that bad 'American' style of sound editing', by which they meant it was choppy, constantly shifting perspective, going from soft to loud etc. The European lecturer taught that a smoother, more linear approach (more musical, really) approach is better. I, of course thought he was nuts. There are cases for a very contrasty style and cases for a more over-arching style, within the same movies even. Depends on what you're trying to do. But if there is a difference in approach to sound, I would say in general that the European and Japanese cinema have used sound more subjectively (Polansky, Godard, Kurosawa, Lean), while the American style often sticks to the literal. The challenge to me is figuring out when to be literal, and when to be subjective, and how to move between the two. Sound can be difficult to talk about since its effects are almost subconscious, but that makes for interesting discoveries.

Discussions with James Bernard

Dated 1998

Heather Emmett: Following on from our letters I'd really like you to talk about the ways you construct different elements of fear through your orchestrations and use of timbre.

James Bernard: Obviously the first thing I would say, it sounds a bit obvious but I would think to avoid concord. You want to get harmonies that are sort of disturbed and never resolve and that's why a lot of my scores, if you are analysing them carefully, you will see whole patches of them are atonal really – in no particular key. And you keep it like that and think, 'oh this is going on too long I'd better do something!' But you really need to keep it going on a knife-edge for long stretches sometimes.

Whereas if you were writing a piece, as say a piece of concert music, you would need to *resolve* it, resolve the harmonies at some stage, but in a long section where you are depicting fear, you really need these kind of disturbing harmonies. A single line is often very good too, you know one solo instrument with a slightly sinister melodic line can be extremely effective. There are a whole lot of devices. I'm sure you would agree *percussion* is very important, it seems basic but drums carefully and well-used can be very exciting and create a great sort of tension. Then there are all the very different effects for instance the string effects, like tremolo and tremolo *sul ponticello* near the bridge of the instrument which gives that sort of high, glassy sound.

HE: And the brass?

JB: You would usually want to mute the brass and then play it loud because it gives a much nastier noise.

If your are using horns, which I don't always use, but if you are using horns to have them overblown. I think it's called *geschtopped...* and they can either stop them by hand and then blow. I am not a brass player at all but I think if they are doing this effect in this way that they have to aim at a note higher than what you have written. It comes out at the note it's supposed to but with a nasty raspy sound, or you could have them stopped with a mute and then blown hard which has I suppose more or less the same effect. I think probably the hand stopping is more effective.

I think it's also important to tell the players–although of course when I started out I felt far too shy, I was always in awe of all the orchestral players because they were all so brilliant and I used to think I can't *believe* that they are playing my music.

When I started they were wonderful players, I mean they still are but in the days when I started with Hammer, we'd have Leon Goosens who was one of the great oboe players of the century, we might have him on first oboe. We might have Jack Brymer one of the great clarinetists on first clarinet and Hugh Bean who was leader of one of the big orchestras for years, he might easily be the first violin and so I was always in awe of them.

But if you can, you want to tell them the sort of idea you are trying to get at. I think it helps because then they cooperate, if you say I want a really *nasty noise* here, a sort of frightening noise and then they will try to do it.

HE: You've written scores purely for strings...

JB: Yes, my three first scores were all strings, I'll tell you how that happened. Before I started to do film music I was writing quite a lot of music for radio plays. This was back in the early fifties you see and so TV hadn't really started up again in England. I mean it had hardly started before the war – I think it just had but it wasn't like everybody had TV in their house, but of course everybody had radio and so radio plays were as important then as plays, or whatever it is on TV nowadays.

In those days the BBC used to commission a lot of specially written scores and I got into doing this. I'd done a score for the *Duchess of Malfi* by Webster. I can't remember the actual date of the period of it but a little way after Shakespeare, but it's a real horror play I mean it's a marvelous play with wonderful poetry. But it is a real horror play, I recommend it – and everybody gets murdered, poisoned and stabbed, it's really appalling. Anyway I'd written this score and John Hollingsworth who was the early music director for Hammer up until when he died, he was a brilliant conductor and he used to conduct the Royal Ballet and he was assistant to Malcolm Sergeant and he did the films as well. I'd got to know him towards the end of my time in the Air Force. He used to conduct the Air Force band and so he was conducting these scores for me for radio and I did a score for the *Duchess of Malfi* and I discussed it with John and I said well I think for the sort of effect we need – we need strings and percussion and we needn't have anything else.

For radio we weren't allowed to have an enormous orchestra, we had to have comparatively small groups and so I wrote this score for strings and percussion which they seemed to like at the BBC. It had a wonderful cast with Paul Schofield, Peggy Ashcroft, you know a lot of the leading actors.

It was soon after that that John Hollingsworth got a telephone call from a great producer at Hammer Films and he said, 'we're in a bit of a spot, because the composer who was going to write the score for our current movie, which is *Quatermass Experiment*, is ill.' So they needed a composer as soon as possible and they asked John have you anybody up your sleeve who might do it. Now John knew I was looking to get into films so he hurried down to Bray Studios and played the tape. We had just started to be able to do the stuff on tape, so this was luckily on tape and he took it to play for them and Tony (Hines) said, 'yes lets ask him to do it, I like it'. So John said 'You've got the job!' (it's a very exciting and frightening moment, ones first film score). And he said to me that given the subject, which as you know is Science Fiction.. strings and percussion are exactly what's needed.

Anyway it seemed to work and everybody was delighted so then they asked me to do their next one which was science fiction again and that was *X The Unknown* and then the third one was *Quatermass 2*, they all came in a little cluster together, so all those things I did as strings and percussion. It seemed to work well for that sort of bleak, horrific science fiction subject.

HE: Why do you think that is?

JB: They are marvelous strings they really are wonderful. I think one could really write almost any kind of score using just strings and it's because they can do so many things. They can sound so romantic, they can sound very jolly and happy, especially if you use some *pizzicato*. They can really do everything.

So that was my first three and it was only when I came to do the *Curse of Frankenstein*, which was my first sort of *Gothic* Horror score that I said to John Hollingsworth, 'I think now I've got my hand in with the strings and percussion you must let me use some other instruments' and he said, 'okay fine'. That was the first score where I used woodwind and brass.

HE: Can you talk through the process?

JB: Yes, well as you know you go through the film, but in those days what I used to do was go down to...I think in those days Hammer had a very good little viewing theatre right in the West End of London in Hammer House, which still exists, though it's not inhabited by Hammer anymore. So we'd either do it there or we'd do it at Bray Studios and it's the composer, the music director, the producer. The producer was usually Tony Hines in those days and he was very good musically, he had a very musical ear and very good constructive ideas about the music. And there would be the editor of the film and the editors assistant and then there would be the sound editor because he knew what all the other sounds would be, I mean we knew where there was dialogue but we didn't always know where there might be tremendous thunder or horses hooves of Dracula's carriage ripping along through the woods and that sort of thing. So he would be there too and you would go through the film reel by reel and stop after every reel and decide where you are going to put the music – which bits of the reel need music.

Of course in those early days I was far too junior, far too nervous about it, I made some suggestions but they took no notice of me really because they were much more experienced at it than I was. They would discuss where they thought the music needed to be and actually in the end I always saw eye to eye with them, they were right. Then it was the job of the assistant editor to note all this down and then he or she had to measure out each section where there was going to be music, exactly where it starts and stops and everything that happens between those two points and then you would get a typed list (cue sheets) for each music cue. 1M1 meaning reel one music one, which was obviously always the title music, or at least it was in those days. The 1M2 which would be the second bit of music in reel one and supposing later in the film music begins with Mina lying in bed restless, tossing and turning and pulling at her night gown, you know because she knows what's going to happen and the music might start there and then suddenly cut to Dracula at the window. So they would right down for you exactly how many feet of film it starts at, how many feet of film it is when you cut to Dracula and each foot of film takes two thirds of a second, so everything can be worked out exactly.

First you decide what the material is that you are going to use for that particular section, with any luck by then you have two or three themes that you are going to use and then you may have some subsidiary themes, a romantic one if possible. So you decide what the material is for each section and then you decide exactly what speed it should go at throughout this particular section. So you decide the speed and well it's easier to say it's sixty beats to a minute because then it's a beat to a second and that often works very well for a slow piece of music. But on the other hand if you double that if it's a fast section and you double it to make it one hundred and twenty to the minute, that is really often not fast enough, which is a nuisance because it would be very easy to work things out as you know, two beats to a second. But if you really need to be going hammer and tongs you need about a hundred and forty four, in my experience.

Once you've decided on the speed the section is to go at, then you work out absolutely mathematically where your sync points are going to go. It may come off the beat, just after the beat on a quaver or something. Then you have to start composing the stuff using the material that you've thought of and making sure that on the points of synchronisation that *what's meant to happen does happen* if the conductor is conducting at *exactly* the tempo that is marked.

As a film conductor, obviously you have to have full control over the orchestra and they must follow you exactly. Some conductors like to have click tracks but I don't think Phillip Martell or John Hollingsworth used them. Maybe just for rehearsing it but they could just sort of feel it in their veins, they would know. It's a great skill as it has to be absolutely precise and there's always a race against time.

HE: What deadlines were you up against?

JB: In those days we did a three hour session and according to the rules of the Musicians' Union, (I don't know if I am up to date on this) but at that time you were not allowed to record more than twenty minutes music in three hours, you could probably have say half an hours overtime. But it was always a bit of a race against time. You might do a section where something might not have worked and you might need to adjust it or do it again. I used to sit in the control room with the sound engineer so I could hear what was going to come through on the recording and then

I could say if something needed changing with the balance or whatever. There wasn't always time to play each one back.

HE: I read somewhere that you had an average of three weeks to complete?

JB: Well yes, a nightmare – *The Legend of the Seven Golden Vampires*. Phil Martell did say on that one 'we've only got *two* weeks.' But he was very helpful. I mean it was a real slog because I'm not a fast composer, but in those days (and I would still do it now if I had to) but you know you would have to work pretty much round the clock. I like to compose late at night.

HE: One thing that's noticeable to me in your scores is that you manage to allow the dialogue to breath. How do you approach that?

JB: Oh I am glad! I think basically what you have to do is to have the music moving very slowly, hardly moving at all. You can have a lot of long chords or just notes creating the tension or what-ever the mood is for the dialogue, or of course you can play a romantic theme very softly. You don't want to have instruments that are going to cut across voices too much, and look for a pause in the dialogue where you can let a phrase swell out and back in again. I think the thing is to not make the music too busy, unless it's something that the ears can quickly get used to, like a background noise almost, to build tension or build romance.

HE: There's a nice example in *Taste the Blood of Dracula.* So if you are wanting to build tension under the dialogue, let's say with percussion...you would bring that motive in early, so that the ear is already used to hearing it before the dialogue enters?

JB: Yes, yes, get it going.

HE: You use *leitmotifs* a lot.

JB: Yes I do.

HE: How do you prevent them from being too repetitive. *The Gorgon* was full of them.

JB: Yes I had several themes.

HE: All connecting people together.

JB: Yes that's right.

I think the thing to do is to use different instrumentation. And sometimes have it high and sometimes low and so forth and like when working with dialogue choose your instrument. If it's a low deep voice, choose a higher instrument. Choose frequencies that aren't fighting against each other.

I actually prefer not to do any music under dialogue, but sometimes you have to do things against your will. The bosses will say 'no we feel it *needs* it'. If a dialogue scene is well acted, which in those cases I think they were I must say, well then I tend to think why do we need music? But I think a lot of directors and producers like to play safe because, well you know yourself how it can help. Ideally though I would rather not.

HE: You do seem to find corners where we can stop and breath. You know when to stop hitting us over the head!

JB: Well I was very lucky with the music directors at Hammer, who felt very similarly to me which is that music is more effective if it's not going on all the time. Wall to wall sound just becomes a background noise. If you choose your places carefully then it can really add something to a film.

PART II

THE SOUND WORLD
of
DARIO ARGENTO

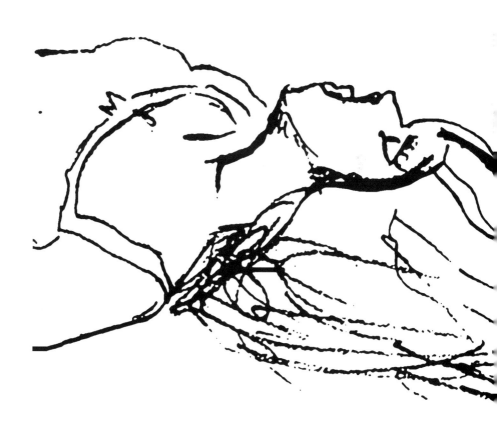

Possibly the closest example to *auditive encoding* can be observed in the use of *leitmotifs* in film music, which typically associate a specific musical theme with a specific character in the text. This practice became commonplace in the genre of horror films where the role of a killer would often be represented by a musical motive. One of the chief exponents of this device was Hammer Horror composer James Bernard and followers of the genre would immediately recognise Bernard's 3-note descending motives that helped characterise the sound of British horror[1].

In one of my discussions with Bernard at his home in Chelsea, he described the ways in which he frequently created themes from the names of films or characters. The descending three–note motive "Drac-u-la" is arguably his most well-known and was used as a signifier for the presence of Dracula, first appearing in *Horror of Dracula* (Terence Fisher, 1958), then again in *Dracula Prince of Darkness* (Terence Fisher, 1965) and again in *Dracula Has Risen From the Grave* (Freddie Francis, 1968). Once this *leitmotif* had been established it began to evolve over Bernard's next two scores, *Taste the Blood of Dracula* (Peter Sasdy, 1970) and *Scars of Dracula* (Roy Ward Baker, 1970). Although the motive itself has undergone thematic development, it remains unmistakably that of Dracula. Through repeated listening and viewing the audience becomes aware, either consciously or subconsciously, that the musical motive is related to the killer.

In the same year (1970), Italian Horror pioneer Dario Argento exhibited the first signs of an interesting auteur style, whereby these *motivic* developments can be found in the *sound* track, not just the music score. Following on from his predecessor, Mario Bava, Argento adopted a style of film-making that drew inspiration from Italian *giallo* mystery novels.

Characterised by a distinctive visual vocabulary that takes a somewhat fetishistic view of murder, *giallo* films are typified by recurring characters: "haunted protagonists touched by madness and irrational violence, psychopaths whose depredations are as bizarre as they are brutal" (McDonagh, 1994).

Argento's first *giallo* film, *L'uccello dalle piume di cristallo* (aka *The Bird with the Crystal Plumage*, 1970) is a carefully executed thriller with an intelligent plot incorporating an inventive system of codes. In keeping with McDonagh's (1994) description of the classical thriller as "planting clues where the astute viewer can find and make use of them", Argento positioned coded messages in both the visuals and the sound to produce clues within the narrative as to the location and identity of the killer. Clues for the attentive viewer to decode in his or her own investigation of the crime.

The Bird with the Crystal Plumage introduced a number of both visual and auditory signifiers that Argento would go on to employ throughout his later films. For example visually, black gloves, (which are part of the iconography of *giallo* films), were shown to be synonymous with the killer and it is in this film that we can see signs of Argento's first experimentation in linking the killer with water. Meanwhile, in the soundtrack we are given clues that help to unveil both the location and identity of the killer. The former is achieved within the narrative as the eventual recognition of the sound of a rare bird, heard on a recording of a telephone call made by the killer, helps to pinpoint the apartment where the murderer lives.

While the narrative leads us to believe that the killer is a man, this is at odds with the soundtrack as, throughout the film, whenever the killer is about to strike, a pleasurable female voice can be heard in the soundtrack, seemingly at odds with the visuals. The reason for this becomes apparent right at the end of the film when the killer is unmasked as a woman, and the wife of the man who had confessed to the murders. The clue had been in the soundtrack all along.In his following films, Argento can be seen to experiment more and more with the idea of using various systems of coded messages in order to communicate with the viewer, and even to confuse them. Argento's use of coding is well documented by McDonagh (1994) who states that although "the terms may differ from film to film, Argento's work is suffused with evidence of a variety of systems in operation, and it entices – even dares – the viewer to enter into a dialogue with the filmic text[2]".

However, McDonagh's otherwise fascinating study of Argento's work, does not raise or discuss the director's consistent use of sound as a signifier. Frequently collaborating with the Anzellotti brothers for Foley and sound effects, Argento enriches his films with soundtracks that not only display interesting crossovers between the use of music and sound – with rock/jazz fusion band Goblin providing some of the sound effects – but which, more importantly, clearly exhibit the use of sound as a form of encoding.

By setting up signifiers that are repeated throughout Argento's films, the viewer is exposed to a system of encoding where a particular sound forms associations with a particular event or character. In some cases this use of sound is so carefully executed that we are able to use it to unmask the killer.

The repetitive use of sound in relation to a particular image sets up a coded message whereby we retain the meaning or function of a sound. When the sound is repeated with or without the image, we continue to associate the sound with that particular character, event or location.

There is a strong psychological basis for such a system of encoding as demonstrated in experiments conducted by Pavlov (1927) into the phenomenon he called 'classical conditioning'. Through his experiments with dogs, Pavlov discovered that "a neutral stimulus [can be] paired with a stimulus that elicits a reflex or other response until the neutral stimulus alone comes to elicit a similar response." (Bernstein, Roy, Srull, Wickens, 1988).

In my interview with Michel Chion[3], we discussed the use of *auditive encoding* within the context of Argento's films and he agreed "Yes, everything can be coded. Like Pavlov, an association between two different things, if repeated, becomes a code. Films are able to create associations, as in life, so when one element is repeated the other is expected".

WATER: BRINGER OF DEATH

In conditioning the viewer to a neutral stimulus that sets up an association with a killer and the act of murder, Argento's (and the Anzellotti's) favoured device was the sight and sound of water, exemplified in his film *Profondo Rosso* (aka *Deep Red*, 1975). Although we can find examples of an association between the killer and water in *The Bird with the Crystal Plumage* (1970), it was not until *Deep Red* that its use as a signifier became marked. It is important to note that the use of sound is inseparable from the filmic image in *Deep Red* and so, if we are to fully grasp the system of encoding employed by Argento, both must be discussed in detail. In my interview with Michel Chion he agreed, explaining that "sound cannot be separated from the images by an abstract decision because when you have rhythm in the image and rhythm in the sounds they are combined like in music...you must not separate the image from sound, it's the whole".

Whilst McDonagh recognised that visually Argento's films are openly coded, she did not carry this theory into the use of sound. Interestingly she spoke of "the curious disjunction between soundtrack and image (principally a matter of music so out of line with the imagery as to be bizarre)."[4] Yet to my mind, it is the two together that set up a system of encoding within the narrative, so that the one cannot fully be understood without a critical appreciation of the other.

In the opening minutes of *Deep Red* we are presented with a scene that not only sets up the sound of water as a signifier for murder but also foreshadows later events in the narrative. The film begins at a Parapsychology Conference in Rome, where clairvoyant Helga Ullman speaks about her telepathic powers. As she describes and demonstrates her abilities to her audience a terrible pain suddenly overcomes her. *"There's something... someone"* she exclaims, and in the music score we hear pizzicato strings emulating the sound of dripping water before cutting to a point of view shot from where the murderer is sitting. *"I don't know what it is myself. I'm sorry. Forgive me. It was...I can't explain it, something strange, like a knife entering my flesh. Please forgive me. It's better now, thank you"*. The camera cuts to a close-up of her face as she shouts once more in pain and as she speaks of sensing death, a presence, of having entered into contact with a perverse mind *"its thoughts are of death"*, off screen we hear the sound of water being poured into a glass. Ullman is then passed the water and through an extreme close-up we see her immediately expel the water from her blood red lips, as though she is aware of its impurity. At the same time, the sound of water is exaggerated. This scene is alluded to after her murder when we are given a close-up of saliva running from her mouth, indeed all the murder victims expel water from their mouths, in some form or other, in connection with being killed[5].

As Helga is framed against the blood-red background she points in the direction of the killer and continues to speak of the house where the original murder took place. As she does so she mentions *"that nursery rhyme"*, which is played *acousmatically* preceding each attack – first heard in a flashback to the original murder scene during the opening credits. Throughout this sequence the music works around her voice as if it is part of the orchestration, all the time drawing us in and focusing our attention on those elements that will form a coded language within the narrative. A hand-held point-of-view shot tells us that the murderer is getting up and leaving the room, yet we hear no Foley until the last three footsteps as the killer approaches a door marked 'WC'. The importance of this is realised later when we discover there are two killers. A close-up shot of three footsteps as the killer enters Helga's apartment tells us this is the same person we saw at the Parapsychology conference who entered the WC. This opening scene serves to set up two main auditory signifiers: a) it introduces a link between water and death and b) Helga mentions the killer's musical leitmotif, the nursery rhyme – which is played on a reel-to-reel tape deck preceding each murder. Visually it raises the question as to whether there are two murderers. Firstly, we have been taken in the direction of the WC by a point-of-view shot, suggesting the killer has already left in that direction, but we are then drawn out the way we entered the scene, through thick red curtains by another point-of-view shot.

The association between the sound of water and the killer really becomes established in the scene that follows. Situated in the WC, the sound of footsteps leads us to a close-up of the wash basin. We hear the sound of a woman about to be sick and at the point where we hear her start vomiting water simultaneously gushes from the tap. A series of five successive shots of running water juxtaposed against the sound of this woman being sick ensure the creation of a strong audio-visual link between the two. As the sound of water continues we see an extreme close-up of someone fastening a black leather glove – a signifier followers of Argento would immediately recognise as denoting 'a killer' – and so an association is formed between water, woman and killer. In my interview with Chion he explained "Water is often associated to something maternal; it is life and death at the same time...In some cases water can suggest purity, childhood...it all depends on the context."

Chion's view on the symbolism of water can be applied in both its forms to the diegesis of *Deep Red*. Water has already linked us to the killer, who we now know to be female (a notion upheld in abstract intercutting sequences that give us glimpses into the killer's psyche and show an extreme close-up of someone applying heavy black eyeliner), and as the twisted logic of *Deep Red* develops this woman's son later kills to protect his mother.

The use of water by Argento functions to communicate information to the *viewer* rather than the on-screen characters to whom its presence has no apparent meaning. With the opening scenes of the film having established a clear association between the element of 'water' and 'death' it now follows that the sight and sound of water alone acts as a signifier for a killer. For example, when the protagonist investigating the murders, Marc Daly, enters the house where the original murder took place, although the killer is not physically evident, the inherent danger of the place is communicated to the audience when Marc enters the flooded basement. To emphasise the importance of this shot the camera then pulls back through the door so that what we focus on is the sound of Marc splashing around in the water, although we can no longer see him. Similarly, when Marc and his reporter girlfriend Gianna enter the school attended by the killer's son as a child, the *sound* of running water precedes a sequence of shots in the toilets showing water gushing out of a toilet, running freely from one tap and dripping from another. We soon discover that the son is in the building with them and has already killed one of Marc's colleagues to prevent his Mother's identity as the murderer from being discovered. The danger is realised as both are attacked, resulting in Gianna being stabbed, though the wound proves not to be fatal.

This scene provides an example of the way that Argento uses the intensity of sound to communicate with the viewer in signifying the victim's level of danger. For example, dripping water is less dangerous than free-flowing water. By showing us a close-up of two taps, as Marc and Gianna enter the school, where one tap drips and the other gushes water we are given a clue that suggests one of these characters is in more immediate danger than the other. Earlier in the film, whilst the murder of Helga Ullman was taking place we cut outside to a conversation between Marc and the killer's son, and second murderer,

Carlo who are framed against a large fountain that gushes forth water – signifyng the attack on Helga. When we cut back to this same location following the murder the fountain is completely dry, indicating that there is no longer any danger. When we discussed the use of repetition in horror films, Chion explained that in cinema the repetition of a sound is often related to death. As an example he quoted Brian De Palma's film *Blow Out* (1981), where the suggestion of death was created by the repetition of a sound that occurred each time the killer committed a murder. It is frightening, he says, precisely because of the repetition.

One of Argento's later films, *Tenebre* (1982), can be seen to draw parallels with *Deep Red* in its incorporation of two murderers and the use of flashbacks to provide an insight into the mind of the killer. *Tenebre* goes on to develop the use of water as a signifier but its use adopts two separate forms so that there is a clear distinction between the signifier of water in relation to each killer. On the one hand, the repeated use of bubbling water, in conjunction with a series of flashbacks, takes us into the mind of novelist, Peter Neal, whose motive for murder stems from a repressed anger toward women. The other killer, Christiano Berti, commits murder as an act of cleansing and purification towards those characters he sees as displaying aberrant behaviour. Berti therefore, is represented by a much more naturalistic use of water, for example: running taps, a water sprinkler and the sound of a swimming pool in his garden. Through Argento's previous association with the signifier of water we again question characters, locations and mental states.

BEWARE THE RAPTUS

Whilst water signifies the presence of a killer to the film's audience, *"that nursery rhyme"* mentioned by Helga Ullman at the conference, as she echoes the killer's mind, functions within the plot by alerting the characters to imminent danger. In keeping with the form of omniscient narration employed by *Deep Red* – in that the audience sees, hears and knows more than any or all of the characters – the viewer has already heard the nursery rhyme

70

accompany the original murder during a flashback inserted in the opening credits. Therefore it has immediately become associated with danger. Having already told us about the link between the nursery rhyme and death, Ullman is naturally perturbed by its *acousmatic* appearance in her apartment and rightly so as she is attacked and killed once the music has stopped.

This children's song functions *anempathetically* as it seems incongruous with the anxiety exhibited by each victim as he or she mentally struggles to identify the source of the music. Because it is used as *acousmatic* sound, in that its source is not seen, the characters, the victims, do not know where the nursery rhyme is coming from and so are unable to locate the killer by it. It is only later in the film that we discover the music to be coming from what Chion would call an 'acousmachine'[6] – a reel-to-reel tape player held by the killer. The scene where this occurs is important for another reason as it provides an auditory clue about the identity of the killer.

As Marc sits composing at his piano, we see a point-of-view shot of the killer walking across the roof of his apartment. His/her steps are deliberate and in time with Marc's piano playing, as if giving us a clue that the killer is musical. In fact both killers are musical and we are frequently given clues to this through the way the music score interacts with the visuals. For example, during the murder of Helga Ullman, a frantic piano part in the music serves to represent the killer's point-of-view. Also, in a later murder scene, a piano motif exaggerates the symbolic gesture of the camera zooming in on three books whose spines clearly allude to piano keys. Upon hearing the nursery rhyme Marc looks up and the camera cuts to an extreme close-up of the tape player. However, we cannot say that the music now married to its source has been totally de-acousmatized, only partly so it does not yet reveal the killer with whom it is inextricably linked.

According to Chion this partial de-acousmatization process functions to "put off until another time and place the true unveiling of the acousmetre" [7] as a "sound or voice that remains acousmatic creates a mystery of the nature of its source, its properties and its powers"[8].

For the astute audience, however, it is at this point that an assumption can be made regarding the killer's identity. We have already received enough information to decode the killer as being female, initially in the association between running water, black gloves and the sound of a woman vomiting; then in the inter-cutting shots that link black-gloved hands with an extreme close-up shot of eyeliner being applied. Now, we hear the killer deliberately walking in time with Marc's piano playing and this, taken in conjunction with the music score – where the piano part is used subjectively to suggest the killer's point-of-view – allows us to decode the killer as being Carlo's mother. We know there are only three people within the narrative who are musical: Marc, Carlo and Carlo's mother, and they are all pianists. We also know that neither Marc nor Carlo were involved in the murder of Helga Ullman as we cut away to a conversation between the two whilst Helga is being attacked. Therefore,we are left with Carlo's mother. Had we ignored the important clues encoded into the soundtrack we could not have made this deduction so early in the film's storyline.

The narrative explanation regarding the function of the nursery rhyme is given by a colleague of Helga Ullman's, Professor Giordani who, upon hearing a recording of the nursery rhyme played by Marc, provides a psychological explanation of its use:

"Someone who kills with such fury, most certainly acts when over-come by a 'raptus'. Under ordinary circumstances this person can seem perfectly normal, like you or me. To be able to kill he needs the conditions to be right, for his madness to surface...a particular time of day, or day of the week Maybe wearing certain clothes. In other words something that recreates the same images...that in the past were the conditions that caused his trauma".

As we have previously discussed, water alerts us to the presence of the killer, but the nursery rhyme, the murderer's *raptus*, tells us that an attack is happening now. It therefore functions in a different way. According to the psychological theories of Skinner, the nursery rhyme acts as an *operant* – a response that operates on the environment in some way. For example, when a child says, "Momma I'm hungry" and is then fed, the child has emitted an operant response that determines when a particular stimulus (in this case food) will appear. Similarly, touching a hot barbecue grill is an operant that results in a painful burn (Bernstein et al, 1988). In comparison, the playing of the nursery rhyme will result in murder. We therefore have two main auditory signifiers of extreme danger functioning within the narrative: the sound of water; and the killer's *raptus*. Yet a third signifier also exists in the element of wind, which appears in an abstract rather than naturalistic form in *Deep Red*.

WATCHER IN THE WIND

Although the sound of wind is also used to represent the killer it represents him/her in a more thoughtful state of mind, hiding or watching his victims for example. It is interesting to note, therefore, that when we hear the sound of wind we do not hear the *raptus*. The first time this device is used is after the Parapsychology conference when Ullman describes what she experienced to professor Giordani. The killer is hiding to the right of the camera and Ullman is alerted to his/her presence by the sound of wind. Female vocal effects are also present in the mix (providing a further clue that the killer is female) along with the tinkling of a music box. The murderer does not attack but lurks in the background watching and listening. This happens again as Marc researches a book in the library and the killer watches him from across the room. In both cases we do not see the killer but the repeated use of this device serves to associate the sound of wind with the killer watching. It is important to note that in both these cases the onscreen action is located indoors so that the sudden appearance of the sound of wind is highly *acousmatic* in being so far out of place. This unnatural feeling is further heightened due to the synthetic quality of the sound, which was provided by the writers of the music score, Goblin using a Minimoog synthesizer.

Although wind as a single signifier represents less immediate danger than water or the *raptus*, when used together they become stronger. It is no surprise therefore that the killer's most frenzied attack uses all three signifiers. One of the murder victims in the narrative is an author who had written of the dark and ghostly tale surrounding the murderer's abandoned house (this was the book Marc was researching in the library). Prior to her murder we see a sequence of shots where the killer's heavily eyelinered eye is rapidly intercut with an exterior high angle shot of the author, Amanda Righetti's house.

As Amanda enters a room she sees a doll with a noose around its neck hanging from the ceiling, a visual signifier used throughout which not only represents the immediate presence of a killer, but also foreshadows the death of the murderer, Carlo's mother, as she is decapitated by her own necklace. We hear the 'watching' theme comprised of synthetic wind, music box and maddened female voices, this time joined by the sound of dripping water, all *acousmatic* and much more intense than we have heard any of these elements before. The combination of the four elements crescendos into a powerful torrent of wind as the camera pans left to reveal the killer's eye staring from the shadows. These two auditory and visual signifiers of the killer watching become momentarily meshed, but the wind is now powerful and wild and, having been merged with the signifier of water, is now dangerous.

This intense watching theme breaks off suddenly as we cut to an extreme close-up of the killer's black-gloved hand holding a tape player and immediately the *raptus* starts, signifying that the waiting and watching is over, it's killing time. After a brief period of silence the frenzied piano and guitar music begins and we have a scene that presents a culmination of the water and wind motives distinctive association with the killer. This time, their use is not pre-narrative or off-screen, but onscreen and forming part of the action. As Amanda lies unconscious on the bathroom floor, having been attacked by the killer, we are given a lingering close-up of saliva running from her mouth, just as we saw when Helga was killed. The killer sets the bath tap running and we witness an interplay of visual themes, cutting between running saliva and running water. A series of close-up shots of the mirrored walls steaming up informs us not only of the temperature of the water but also foreshadows the important role the mirrored surface will later play. The music stops as the killer plunges Amanda's head into the boiling water to kill her. The splashing of the water and Amanda's occasional cry are the only sounds we can hear. As she lies dying on the bathroom floor she writes a message into the steamed up wall with her finger. However, in a continuation of the watching motif, the window blows open and a light, naturalistic, wind can be heard to fill the room, dispersing the condensation and with it the victim's message.

As mentioned before, Argento's use of coding within his films also serves to confuse the spectator, to throw us off the scent, so to speak. Visually he uses a number of devices that prompt us to question characters, to make us wonder if this character or possibly that one could be the killer. For example, in *Deep Red* we know that the killer is a woman who wears heavy eyeliner, so Argento has all the female characters made up in this way, from Carlo's mother, to the reporter Gianna Brezzi and even Carlo's transvestite lover.

Argento is also fond of having characters display expressions that seem inappropriate and suspicious when taken in context. For example, when Marc goes to the old house and discovers a body bricked up behind a false wall we see him knocked unconscious, presumably by the killer. We then cut to an exterior shot of Marc lying in Gianna's lap while the house is on fire. The way the camera slowly tilts up to reveal Gianna's face and her impassive stare makes us suspicious of her innocence, a device earlier used by Argento in *The Bird with the Crystal Plumage*. Argento also has a fondness of associating the colour red with various decoy killers. Always, however, the truth regarding the identity of the killer can be discovered by listening critically to the soundtrack. The very incongruence of the way Argento positions sound against image should drive us to seek an implicit meaning in the sound, beyond what we are seeing.

SYMBOLIC ROOTS

Argento's use of natural elements in his system of encoding can be traced back to his predecessor, Mario Bava, whose film *La Maschera Del Demonio* (*The Mask of Satan*, 1960) exhibited the use of both water and wind to signify a killer, though to a much lesser degree than Argento utilised this device. According to Jung's dream theory and his notion of archetypal iconography, it is possible that natural elements are frequently chosen as signifiers since the symbolism of water, wind etc. is not only relevant to us as individuals, but rather these are images that we share from previous exposure or our collective unconscious. Jung's own archetype of water corresponds to its use as a signifier by Argento in *Deep Red*, and also to Chion's description of the association of water, as Jung saw water as symbolising the great mother.

It is also possible to follow a clear religious link to the way certain sounds have become potent signifiers. In short, the Apocalypse tells the story of the end of the earth. There are frequent associations throughout the text that link the sound of natural elements to death, for example: (Revelation 8:8) "the second angel blew his trumpet, and something like a great mountain, burning with fire was thrown into the sea, and a third of the sea became blood, a third of the living creatures in the sea died...". Again, (Revelation 8:10) "the third angel blew his trumpet and a great star fell from the heavens, blazing like a torch, and it fell on a third of the rivers and on the fountains of water...and many men died of the water, because it was made bitter"[9].

If we are to take on board that human sin corrupts nature, a sinful and unrepentant society must be a hazardous contaminant to the planets natural elements. It is possible, therefore, that natural elements when used to symbolise a killer are actually symbolising a lack of rational control, which is clearly evidenced in Argento's work. For example. the sound of dripping and running water symbolising Carlo and his mother in *Deep Red* and the sound of bubbling water taking us into Neal's mental state in *Tenebre* etc.

Religious symbolism is not usually blatant in Argento's work, as is often the case with many other horror film directors. Crosses burning the foreheads of Vampires, or the Holy Church intervening with blessed sacraments could never be considered part of Argento's style. The evil portrayed by Argento is usually that of the human mind. Having said that, *Tenebre's* name itself is the name of a service held by the Catholic Church, whereby the church is gradually drawn into darkness. Similarly as *Tenebre's* stark mise-en-scene progressively dims, we too are drawn into the ever increasing darkness of Peter Neal's mind.

Right: Dario Argento & Claudio Simonetti with Goblin.

The use of sound in providing auditory signifiers that present information about the killer before their identity has been revealed has been testified to by Chion (1994), who states that "It's fairly common in films to see evil, awe-inspiring, or otherwise powerful characters introduced through sound before they are subsequently thrown out to the pasture of visability, de-acousmatized".

So far, we have seen Argento employ a number of auditory devices that signal the presence of a killer long before his or her identity is made known, but nowhere is this delay in the de-acousmatization process more apparent than in his 1977 film *Suspiria*. The story

tells of a young American dancer, Suzy Banyon, who travels to Germany to study at an exclusive Academy in the Black Forest.

After one of the students and her companion are hideously murdered, Suzy and her ill-fated friend Sarah make the chilling discovery that the Academy is run by a coven of witches, at the head of which is an ancient Black Queen, Helena Marcos, long ago thought to have been killed in a fire.

In *Suspiria*, Argento's use of auditory signifiers not only provides clues about the killer's identity, but manifests the killer as a true *acousmetre* – an embodiment of Chion's 'three powers and one gift' classification:

"First, the acousmetre has the power of 'seeing all'; second, the power of 'omniscience'; and third, the 'omnipotence' to act on the situation. Let us add that in many cases there is also a gift of 'ubiquity' – the acousmetre seems to be able to be anywhere he or she wishes." (Chion, 1994).

To symbolise the omniscient power of the witches Argento used sound, in the form of vocal effects, added by Goblin[10]. This device enabled the 'presence' of the witches to be evident without them physically appearing onscreen. Throughout the film we hear a wordless montage of voices, during moments of anxiety, consisting of vocal effects such as laboured breathing, sighing, snoring and gasping, even the sound of someone blowing on a microphone all overlaid, one on top of the other. Psychologically, sounds such as these serve to make the viewer uncomfortable as they represent an unusual closeness to someone or something unfamiliar. This is further exaggerated by their ambiguous nature as they occupy a space somewhere between the realms of onscreen and off-screen sound. The viewer is privileged in hearing a danger that the onscreen characters cannot hear, just like the camera might cut-away to show the audience an imminent danger the onscreen characters cannot see.

An example of these vocal effects can be found in the first of three murder scenes. As our protagonist, Suzy Banyon, is driven away from the Dance Academy she sees a young woman, Pat, running through the forest. As she runs toward a friend's apartment we hear her run through a puddle of water, the sound of which is exaggerated, prompting those who have seen Argento's previous films to be on the alert following this well-established signifier of death. Alone in a room in her friend's apartment, Pat is clearly disturbed as a window blows open and a violent sound of wind fills the room (leading up to this the room has been lit to focus our attention on laundry blowing around in the dark outside the window). Through prior exposure in earlier films, the astute viewer has already been primed to decode this as "the killer watching". Yet here, this signifier undergoes a transition, a metamorphosis, as a point-of-view shot from outside the window replaces the sound of wind with laboured heavy breathing, gasps, sighs and other vocal effects, which intensify in both volume and density before the music cue cuts in, and continue as Pat is attacked and killed. From this point on it is the sound of this breathing montage that alerts us to the presence of the witches 'watching' the unsuspecting characters. The signifying presence of wind is not given up completely however, but is used as more of a secondary signifier and in a much more naturalistic form than that provided by Goblin in *Deep Red* (1975) and later in *Tenebre* (1982), although here again, the sound of wind is synthetic. In my interview with Claudio Simonetti[11], he explained:

"The wind you hear in *Suspiria* was made by a Minimoog. Sometimes we mixed it with strange noises, for example, the crushing of a plastic cup in front of the microphone, and sometimes we blended this with the whispers. And so the noise became part of a music. The music part of a sound!"

Argento took the unusual step of partially *de-acousmatizing* this strange breathing within the first half of his film by mixing a clearly onscreen vocal sound in with it, the source of which is identified by one of the characters. Following an infestation of maggots, all the dance students are called to sleep in the main practice hall. As the lights go out the mise-en-scene remains in vivid colour – the white sheets used to separate male and female students now bathed in red light. As the girls lie awake gossiping, their voices do not remain panned central to the image, but rather follow the acoustic space of the characters – hard left for the taunting classmates, central for Suzy and hard right for Sarah speaking beside her.

This widening of the acoustic space serves to isolate the girls and heighten their vulnerability. It also opens out the acoustic space in preparation for the vocal effects that follow. The sound of heavy breathing and sighing, heard in association with Pat's murder, alerts us to the presence of danger, signifying the witches' ability to be everywhere, to see everything as it moves around the acoustic space.

Mixed in with the overlaid montage of vocal effects, we hear a suggestion of snoring. As the audience is already aware of the danger encoded in this breathing motive, the students' vulnerability is heightened by means of a high-angle view that pans over them. A silhouette appears on the curtain that hangs directly behind Suzy and her friend Sarah and, as the music score builds tension, this ghostly figure proceeds to lie down like a wandering soul returning to its tomb.

The music, supplied by Goblin, heightens the girls' fear. With its sustained vowels – similar to the cries and wails associated with Greek tragedy theatre – the music provides a dark chorus as the camera zooms in on the mysterious figure behind them. The music and vocal effects then fade out rather abruptly, focusing our attention on the sound of snoring, emanating from the figure behind the curtain. This, Sarah identifies as belonging to the Directress of the Dance Academy and she recounts to Suzy in great detail having heard this strange, unearthly snore after spending a night in one of the guest rooms at the Academy. The following morning she was informed that the Directress had visited the Academy and had slept in the room next to hers.

"*You see so I know she's the Directress*", Sarah exclaims. Even in the way she is visually presented to us the Directress conforms to the properties of the *acousmetre* – a mysterious character who is typically "hidden behind curtains, in rooms or hideouts" (Chion, 1994).

It is because she remains veiled by the curtain that she is only partially *de-acousmatized* by Sarah naming her, and by the audience's realisation that the strange breathing sounds they have been experiencing are connected with this figure behind the curtain. It is the sounds that represent the Directress and her coven that dominate the offscreen space of *Suspiria*.

VOICE BEHIND THE CURTAIN

In his article Technology and the Aesthetics of Film Sound (1988), John Belton states that the "perceptual process of ... attempting to identify sound can, through a system of delays that postpone the synchronisation of sound and source, be manipulated to create suspense...calling attention to sound as a device by playing with our perception of it." We have already seen Argento use this device in *Deep Red* where the nursery rhyme, or *raptus*, preceding each murder creates an air of suspense precisely because its source is visually excluded from the screen. Subsequently, the first few times it occurs the viewer struggles to place it as either offscreen or even non-diegetic in origin. Yet, whereas the source of the nursery rhyme, a tape deck, is soon revealed and thereafter included onscreen, the breathing sounds in *Suspiria* remain *acousmatic* right up to the final moments of the film, sustaining the suspense up until the last. It is not until the end of the film that de-acousmatization takes place when Suzy follows the narrative clues that lead her to Helena Marcos, the Directress, behind a labyrinth of corridors. In an attempt to hide from the witches' servant, a mute, Suzy enters Marcos' room by accident. She hears the familiar snoring sound and from this we know she is with the Directress, who we then see is asleep, once again, behind a curtain[12]. The very presence of having a mute character in the film is significant as Chion (1999), regards the mute as possessing similar powers to that of the *acousmetre*. He also considers the mute as "guardian of the secret" and, he says, "we are accustomed to him serving in this way".

Therefore the inclusion of a mute character clues us into the fact that there is a secret, a notion that holds true in *Suspiria* as we realise that the infamous, and unseen, Directress is in fact the ancient Black Queen, Helena Marcos, long ago believed to have been killed.

As the Directress identifies herself as Helena Marcos we hear laughing voices interwoven with her own that continue through the scene and allude to the montage of breathing sounds heard throughout the narrative that signify the Directress and her coven of witches. De-acousmatization consists of an unveiling process and Suzy achieves this literally as she pulls back the curtain to reveal Marcos (although at first, the witch remains invisible until a flash of lightening reveals an outline of her body). Once unveiled, the voice finds itself attributed to and confined to a body, dooming the acousmetre to the fate of ordinary mortals. De-acousmatization roots the acousmetre to a place and says "here is your body, you'll be there and not elsewhere" (Chion, 1999) instantly dispossessing the acousmetre of its aforementioned mysterious powers of seeing all, omniscience, omnipotence and ubiquity. This is demonstrated in the apparent ease with which Suzy kills the Directress and in destroying the acousmetre, with its mass of vocal effects signifying her coven, the remaining witches are also rendered powerless. As explained in the narrative by Professor Milius, *"the coven is like a serpent its strength rests with its leader, that is, with its head. A coven deprived of its leader is like a headless cobra – harmless"*.

GREAT WALL OF SOUND

The entire sound world of *Suspiria* is claustrophobic in essence. In many places we experience a wall of sound that is uncomfortable in the way it crowds the acoustic space, pressing in on the main dialogue. The most prominent example of this can be found in the dance studio sequences, where the noise of the girls chattering and giggling provides a constant and unbroken blanket of sound that seems somewhat unnatural in its closeness to the spectator. The significance of this becomes apparent later on, however, as the *acousmatic* use of the sound of female whispering, chattering and giggling becomes an auditive motive associated with the killer that signifies her victims. We hear it, for example, before Sarah decides to follow the sound of the teachers' footsteps, who she suspects of being witches, to find out where they go each night. The same motive is heard later in the scene as a mysterious figure opens a box containing a knife, the murder weapon used to kill Sarah. The most notable use of this auditive motive occurs, however, following Sarah's murder, as a concerned Suzy meets up with Sarah's friend, Frank, to see if he knows anything of Sarah's disappearance or her talk of witches.

As they speak outside the Convention Centre we can both see and hear the strong wind that envelops them – which we know to decode as the witches watching the couple. What is of particular interest is the sound of young female voices chattering and giggling mixed in with the wind. We could be forgiven for believing these voices are coming from a gathering of people offscreen, however they do not relate to any of the people we have seen in the initial establishing shot, nor does their tone seem appropriate to the situation. With a little observation we discover them to occupy their own acoustic space and deny any notion of internal logic by which 'the sound flow is apparently born out of the narrative situation itself' (Chion,1994). Though strictly *acousmatic*, in that we cannot see their source, they create a different cognitive impression from voices that we would normally label as 'acousmetres' precisely because of the confusion they create. We find ourselves unable to accept the voices as *acousmatic* and this confusion over how to perceive the sound presumably lies in the visual presence of other characters who are active within the scene. This is an inherent problem when we employ causal listening in that, 'where the source of the sound is not evident, the sound itself constitutes our principle source of information about it' (Chion, 1994). Because of this, causal listening is the most easily influenced and deceptive mode of listening. For example, in this scene there is an unconscious desire to attach the *acousmatic* voices to the people onscreen, an apparent need to explain where they are coming from. This is not possible however, as the female voices once more signify the ever-watchful presence of the Directress and because of the circumstances within which we have heard these chattering voices before, we are coded to relate them to danger. This feeling is strengthened by the subjective use of the camera in this scene as it 'watches' the characters from many different and unsettling viewpoints.

The claustrophobic nature of *Suspiria* is not simply confined to the *sound*-track but was further extended into the music by Goblin, where a fascinating array of vocal effects can be heard. Three predominating themes were used to carry the witches' all-encompassing presence beyond the diegesis and into the realm of the non-diegetic. "That was a Dario request" Simonetti explained, "he said the audience always had to feel the witches' presence during the movie"[13].

First we have the main theme, a fairy-tale like music box piece[14] used to symbolise the Directress and her coven of witches. It is comprised of celesta, acoustic guitar and a strange percussive sound that Simonetti described as Indian tabla mixed with a Minimoog bass sound. Mixed in with this we hear a harsh, guttural, ungendered voice chanting in monosyllabic unison with the melody line on celesta in an almost mocking way. Also, a male voice reciting spoken text, of which most of the words are unintelligible. Finally there is a distorted cry of *"Witch!"* that has been overlaid and occurs throughout the narrative, providing an important auditive clue about the secret contained at the Dance Academy. The second theme consists of bass and acoustic steel guitar and uses male vocal "Aaahs" similar to singing found in Greek tragedy theatre, as discussed in the practice hall scene where we are introduced to the Directress for the first time. This theme is encoded with a higher level of danger than the witches' music box theme as it is generally used to create extreme tension immediately preceding an attack, indicating the witches' psychotic state of mind. Lastly, the third theme is the most potent of all. Used during the attacks on Pat and her friend, the blind pianist – Daniel, and Suzy, this music indicates death. It uses a driving percussive rhythm overlaid with synth pads, fx and a wailing, maddened voice, neither distinctly male or female in origin.

Each theme is extremely repetitive in nature while the latter two pieces seem unrelenting in their use of driving guitar and drums that produce a wall of sound entrapping the onscreen characters.

It is possible to draw comparisons between Argento's use of sound in *Suspiria* and the "umbilical net" adhered to by Chion (1988) as the voice of the mother, woven around the newborn child like a cobweb: "trapped within the suffocating confinement of the mother's voice, the newborn child resembles a prisoner or prey."[15] Chion spoke of the maternal voice enveloping and trapping the foetus in a sinister way, just as the characters in *Suspiria* are trapped by the voice of the Directress in the Dance Academy. An entrapment that is further compounded by the vocal effects spilling into the non-diegetic music score. The appropriateness of Chion's Maternal Voice theory becomes even more apparent when we take into account *Suspiria's* origins in a collection of essays by Thomas De Quincey's entitled *Suspiria de Profundis* (*Sighs from the Depths*), which also inspired Argento's sequel to *Suspiria, Inferno* (1980). These two sources not only explain the identity of Helena Marcos as being one of three witches known as Mater, or Mother Suspiriorum, but also that she is "the Mother of Sighs". De Quincey describes her thus, "Murmur she may but it is in her sleep. Whisper she may, but it is to herself in the twilight. Mutter she does, but it is in solitary places that are as desolate as she is desolate."[16] And so we can understand why it is that the Directress, Helena Marcos, came to be signified by the use of *acousmatic* vocal effects such as breathing, whispering and sighing.

CONCLUSION

We can now appreciate that Argento's use of sound within his films is not so far out of line with the images as critics would have us believe. To overlook the way the soundtrack functions within the narrative is to miss a vital element of the way Argento sets up a system of encoding within his films that communicates a wealth of information to the viewer. Argento employs a series of signifiers within his film soundtracks that aid the astute viewer in his/her role as amateur detective. It is by listening critically to the soundtrack that the identity of the killer is revealed, and it is here that we find clues to the killer's state of mind and the victim's level of danger. We discover a truth not present in the narrative or visuals, where Argento sets up a number of decoy devices that set us questioning the motives of various characters in order to throw us off the scent.

His most favoured device is the sight and sound of water, which is consistently used throughout his films to signify danger through the strong association he creates between the pairing of water and killer. Through repeated use of this device the audience develops an awareness that the sight or sound of water within a scene poses a threat, even if it is merely the sound of a character running through a puddle, as in *Suspiria*. Furthermore, the level of the threat is signified by the intensity of the sound, whether or not it is accompanied by the image of water, as we saw in *Deep Red* that the sound of running water signifies a far greater level of danger than dripping water. For example, a fountain gushes violently with water during one murder scene yet is shown dry once the danger has passed.

Alongside water, Argento also encoded the sound of wind to perform a specific function within the narrative text. The sound of wind is used to signify the killer in a more thoughtful state of mind, watching his or her potential victims. What is of particular importance is the context in which this occurs, as Argento frequently uses wind as an *acousmatic* sound that seemingly comes out of nowhere during scenes shot internally. Where this is the case, the feeling of danger is intensified precisely because the sound of the wind has mysteriously gained access to a place it would not naturally occur. The hypothesis that "anything out of place equals a threat" is a feature of Argento's films where *acousmatic* sounds provide a vehicle through which the unveiling of a killer's identity can be dramatically delayed. By setting up a strong audio-visual association between the sound of an auditive motive and the presence of a killer, Argento is able to articulate the killer's proximity through the use of sound alone. In this respect the killer becomes a true *acousmetre* with the power to be everywhere and see everything without the need to visually appear onscreen-a device showcased by *Suspiria*.

And so we can see that through the process of encoding, Argento affords his audience an omniscient knowledge of vital plot information. This can lead the astute viewer, or more aptly the astute listener, to identify the killer and to know his/her intentions before they are revealed by the narrative. Argento prompts his audience to seek an implicit meaning in the soundtracks of his films beyond what is presented to them visually, which is often misleading. In this way, the audiences of Argento's films are no longer made up of passive consumers but are actively engaged in a dialogue with the filmic text.

FOOTNOTES

[a] Statement by Walter Murch via e-mail.

[b] In contrast, Luciano Anzellotti stated Dario Argento had very precise ideas about the sound effects he wanted and after their first film together sound became a collaboration. Argento was sometimes involved with the making of his sound effects, and on one occasion they spent two full days finding the right sound for a bracelet. (Discussion with Luciano Anzellotti, Rome).

[c] In a discussion with Massimo Anzellotti, he remarked that we are scared by situations such as being in the dark hearing 'boom boom boom'...and that in film, sound can be more frightening than music. 'In real life we don't hear the music, but we do hear the boom boom boom...and we also hear footsteps with reverb in the dark when we are alone.' We summarised that although it's easy to create tension with music, sound effects can be more productive for creating the feeling of fear, because with sound effects you can recreate a familiar situation.

[d] Again we are given a different experience by Luciano Anzellotti who stated, 'it's just that some directors pay more attention to sound effects. Dario Argento is precise.'

[e] Luciano Anzellotti used this technique a great deal in Dario Argento's films. Bringing the audience into the situation by putting us in the killer's shoes. He demonstrated this technique using a leather wallet.

[f] Low Frequency sounds are often used to signify danger.

[1] James Bernard composed the music to over twenty films for Hammer studios and became their most recognised and celebrated composer.

[2] 'Filmic text' is the term Stephen Heath uses to differentiate between that which one views: "the text engaging the action of reception" and "the physical object that is produced over a period of time under a given set of circumstances" – referred to as the 'filmic system'. Heath, S. "Film and System: Terms of Analysis (Part 1)" in Screen, Vol 16 (no.l), p.9.

[3] A transcript of this interview has been provided in part 1.

[4] McDonagh, M.(1994) Broken Mirrors/Broken Minds: The Dark Dreams of Dario Argento, Citadel Press, New York, p25.

[5] This presents a curious irony as Pavlov monitored the salivation rate of dogs in pairing a neutral stimulus, such as a bell, with food so that the dogs came to salivate to the signal, as much as they did the food.

[6] So called because its function is to conceal the *true* unveiling of the *acousmêtre* until a later time

[7] Chion, M. (1999) The Voice In Cinema, Columbia University Press, New York, p35.

[8] Chion, M. (1994) Audio-Vision: Sound On Screen, Columbia University Press, New York, p72.

[9] The Holy Bible, Oxford University Press, Oxford, p202.

[10] Creators of the music score.

[11] A transcript of this interview can be found in Part 1.

[12] The original term *acousmatic* was apparently the name assigned to a Pythagorean sect whose followers would listen to their master speak behind a curtain – so the sight of the speaker would not distract them from the message.

[13] Interview supplied in Part 1.

[14] Possibly referencing *Suspiria's* relationship to Disney's Snow White and the Seven Dwarves

[15] Silverman, K. (1988) *Acoustic Mirror: The Female Voice in Psycho-analysis and Cinema.*

[16] De Quincey, T. (1994) 'Suspiria de Profundis: Levana and Our Ladies of Sorrow', McDonagh, M. *Broken Mirrors/Broken Minds: The Dark Dreams of Dario Argento*, Citadel Press, New York, pl36.

REFERENCES

Belton, J. (1985) 'Technology and Aesthetics of Film Sound' in Belton, J. / Weis, E., Film Sound: Theory and Practice, USA, Columbia University Press, p65.

Bernstein, D.A. / Roy, E. J. / Srull, T.K. / Wickens, C.D. (1988) Psychology, USA, Haughton Mifflin Co. p247–259.

Chion, M. (1999) Audio Vision: Sound on Screen, Gorbman, C. (Ed & Trans), New York, Columbia University Press, pp. 27, 46, 72, 129–131.

Chion, M. (1999) The Voice in Cinema, Gorbman, C. (Trans), New York, Columbia University Press, pp. 19, 28, 35, 96.

De Quincey, T. (1994) 'Suspiria de Profundis: Levana and Our Ladies of Sorrow', in McDonagh, M. Broken Mirrors/Broken Minds: The Dark Dreams of Dario Argento, New York, Citadel Press, p136.

Gregory, R.L. (Ed), (1987) The Oxford Companion to the Mind, Oxford, Oxford University Press, p159.

Heath, S. (1994) 'Film and System: Terms of Analysis (Part 1)' in McDonagh, Broken Mirrors/Broken Minds: The Dark Dreams of Dario Argento, New York, Citadel Press, p18.

McDonagh, M. (1994) Broken Mirrors/Broken Minds: The Dark Dreams of Dario Argento, New York, Citadel Press, pp15–25, 150.

Newman, K. (1996) The BFI Companion to Horror, London, Cassell, pp.25–26.

Oxford University Press, The Holy Bible, UK, Oxford University Press, p202.

Silverman, K. (1988) Acoustic Mirror: The Female Voice in Psychoanalysis & Cinema

RECOMMENDED READING

Belton, J. & Weiss, E. (1985) Film Sound: Theory & Practice. USA., Columbia University Press.

Berger, A.S.A Arthur. (1991) Media Analysis Techniques. USA., Sage Publishing Ltd.

Bernstein, D.A. / Roy, E.J./ Srull, T.K./ Wickens, C.D. (1988) Psychology, USA., Haughton Mifflin Co.

Black, A. (1996) Necronomicon (Book One), The Journal of Horror & Erotic Cinema. London, Creation Books.

Boardwell, D. / Thompson, K. (1997) Film Art. USA, The McGraw-Hill Companies.

Braudy, L. / Cohen, M. / Mast, G. (1974) Film Theory & Criticism: Introductory Readings, 4th Edition, USA., Oxford University Press Inc.

Brown, R.S. (1930, 1957) Overtones & Undertones: Reading Film Music. USA., Famous Music Corporation.

Brown, R.S. (1994) Overtones & Undertones: Reading Film Music. The Regents of the University of California Press.

Chion, M. (1994) Audio Vision: Sound on Screen. Gorbman, C. (Ed & Trans). New York, Columbia University Press.

Chion, M. (1999) The Voice in Cinema. Gorbman, C. (Trans.). New York, Columbia University Press

Collins, A.P. / Collins, J. / Radner, H. (1993) Film Theory Goes to the Movies. New York, The American Film Institute.

Cook, P. (1985) The Cinema Book. London, BFI London.

Donald, J. (1989) Fantasy and the Cinema. London, BFI London.

Dyson, J. (1997) Bright Darkness: The Lost Art of the Supernatural Horror Film. London, Cassell

Edmunson, M. (1997) Nightmare on Mainstreet: Angels, Sadomasochism and the Culture of Gothic. USA, Harvard University Press.

Engler, B. (1991) Personality Theories: An Introduction, 3rd Edition. Boston, Houghton Mifflin & Co.

Geddes & Grosset (1997) Classical Mythology. The Gresham Publishing Co.

Glazier, M. (1979) The Apocalypse: New Testament: Message 22. USA., Veritas Publications in Association with Michael Glazier Inc.

Goleman, D. (1995) Emotional Intelligence: Why It Can Matter More Than IQ. London, Bloomsbury Publishing Plc.

Gregory, R.L. (Ed.) (1987) The Oxford Companion to the Mind, Oxford, Oxford University Press.

Halliwell, L. (1965) Halliwell's Who's Who In The Movies. Walker, J. (Ed). UK., MacGibbon & Kee Ltd.

Hill, A. (1997) Shocking Entertainment: Viewer Response To Violent Movies. UK., Faculty of Humanities, University of Luton by John Libbey Media.

Jung, C.G. (1987) Dictionary of Analytical Psychology, London, Ark.

Jung, C.G. (1971) Dictionary of Analytical Psychology, Bollinger Foundation.

Kennett, F. (1974, 1985) How To Read Your Dreams: Understanding The Secret World Of Sleep. London, Marshall Cavendish Books Ltd.

Larson, R.D. (1996) Music from the House of Hammer: Music in the Hammer Horror Films 1950 -1980. USA., Scarecrow Press Inc.

Maltby, R. (1995) Hollywood Cinema. USA., Blackwood Publishing Ltd.

McDonagh, M. (1991, 1994) Broken Mirrors/Broken Minds: The Dark Dreams of Dario Argento. New York, Citadel Press.

Mendik, X. (1997) "A (Repeated) Time to Die" Delerium: The Essential Guide To Bizarre Italian Cinema Volume 5, ppl6-17.

Newman, K. (1996) The BFI Companion to Horror. London, Cassell.

Oxford University Press, The Holy Bible. UK., Oxford University Press.

Silverman, K. (1988) Acoustic Mirror: The Female Voice in Psychoanalysis and Cinema. Kaja Silverman.

Skal, D.J. (1994) The Monster Show: A Cultural History of Horror. London, Plexus Publishing Ltd.

Sloboda, J.A. (1985) The Musical Mind: The Cognitive Psychology of Music. New York, Oxford University Press.

Sobchack, V. (1987) Screening Space. The American Science Fiction Film. New York, Ungar.

FILMOGRAPHY

Horror of Dracula, 1958. Terence Fisher

The Mask of Satan, 1960. Mario Bava

The Gorgon, 1964. Terence Fisher

Dracula, Prince of Darkness, 1965. Terence Fisher

Dracula Has Risen From the Grave, 1968. Freddie Francis

Taste the Blood of Dracula, 1970. Peter Sasdy

Scars of Dracula, 1970. Roy Ward Baker

The Bird with the Crystal Plumage, 1970. Dario Argento

The Godfather, 1972. Francis Ford Coppola

Deep Red, 1975. Dario Argento

Suspiria, 1977. Dario Argento

Apocalypse Now, 1979. Francis Ford Coppola

Inferno, 1980. Dario Argento

Tenebre, 1982. Dario Argento

Phenomena, 1985. Dario Argento

The Mothman Prophecies, 2002. Mark Pellington

INDEX

T

T1000 47, 48
Tarantino. Quentin 30
Tarkovsky 34
Taste the Blood of Dracula 58, 63, 101
Tenebre 70, 76, 77, 81, 101
Terminator 20, 48
Terminator 2 48, 49
Tetsuo 2 19
train (sound) 20, 21, 22, 23, 34

U

Ulmer, Edgar G. 30

V

Vanzina, Stefano 30
voice 8, 87, 92, 93, 94, 95, 99

W

war 19, 34, 52
Ward Baker, Roy 63, 101
water 7, 10, 14, 16, 18, 23–24, 26, 27, 32, 35, 46, 47, 66–70,
      72–76, 80, 89
Webster 53
What Lies Beneath 14, 47
White Ribbon 42
wind 8, 10, 14, 16, 38, 41, 46–48, 73–76, 80, 81, 85, 89, 90
Wise, Robert 5, 18, 48
witches 31, 38, 79–87

X

Xenakis 41
X The Unknown 54

Z

Zombie 30

Published by Flaithulach

www.flaithulach.co.uk
info@flaithulach.co.uk

Flaithulach Ltd. Registered England & Wales No 6936332
12A High Street
Knaresborough, North Yorkshire HG5 0EQ

Also from Flaithulach

CHANTER AND WHISTLE
The Uilleann Pipe & Whistle Collector's Series
Part 1

A unique selection of transcribed solos and interviews featuring some of the world's finest traditional musicians.

Full Length Solos & Selected Interviews featuring

**Paddy Keenan Leo Rickard John McSherry
Ronan Browne David Power Thomas Keenan**

Published by Flaithulach
ISBN 978-0-9563020-0-7

www.flaithulach.co.uk